# BRITISH RAILWAYS

## PAST and PRESENT

## No 62

**Map of the area covered by this book, showing locations featured or referred to in the text.**

# BRITISH RAILWAYS

# PAST and PRESENT

# No 62

## The Black Country and
## South and East Staffordshire

### John Whitehouse and Geoff Dowling

Past and Present

Past & Present Publishing Ltd

**To Daphne and Irene**
**Thank you for your patience and support**
**during these last few mad months!**

© John Whitehouse and Geoff Dowling

ISBN 978 1 85895 261 1

Past & Present Publishing Ltd
The Trundle
Ringstead Road
Great Addington
Kettering
Northants NN14 4BW

First published in 2010

British Library Cataloguing in Publication Data

A catalogue record for this book is available from the
British Library.

Tel/Fax: 01536 330588
email: sales@nostalgiacollection.com
Website: www.nostalgiacollection.com

Printed and bound in the Czech Republic

# ACKNOWLEDGEMENTS

Particular thanks are due to Phil Waterfield, Ken Woolley, Andrew Bannister, Brian Robbins, Michael Mensing, David C. Williams, Roger Shenton, John Dew, Paul Dorney, John Bucknall, Rob Selvey and Barry Bull for use of their extensive photographic portfolios and for the provision of invaluable information. Richard Tuplin provided valuable assistance with the text, and Andrew Doherty is thanked for his invaluable website of stations (past and present).

WALSALL: In tandem with its importance as a railway centre, Walsall, in its time, has been graced by fine stations. The South Staffordshire Railway opened a temporary station in Bridgeman Street before a far grander affair was constructed on the present site which opened in 1849. An enlargement took place in 1861 and the station was rebuilt in 1872, when the main entrance was transferred from Station Street to Park Street, which gave it a frontage onto one of the main thoroughfares of the town. It had an air of solidity, especially following the erection of an iron and glass canopy covering the entrance. The canopy survived a serious fire in 1916, which led to the opening of a new booking hall in 1923. This was an impressively spacious, circular structure, with a concourse that had oak-panelled walls with Grecian-style pillars to support the roof. The station is seen here in February 1978, with the magnificent canopy still providing that air of importance, although by now the town's only passenger link was the hourly-interval service to Birmingham New Street via Perry Barr

# Contents

In 1978 redevelopment of the entire area was instigated and the station site was incorporated into a new retail shopping centre, called 'The Saddlers Centre' in recognition of the town's principal industry of saddle-making and associated leather manufacturing. The whole station was subsumed within this new development, the entrance to which is now tucked away at the rear of the centre with access either through an arcade of shops or from a rather gloomy corridor leading from Station Street. Marks & Spencer now occupy the site of the old frontage and booking hall. There was talk of the old station being saved for posterity and reassembled elsewhere, but this has not happened. The location can be determined by Station Street, which diverges to the right. *Both JW*

WEDNESBURY CENTRAL: Black Country contrast – in this busy scene viewed from the footbridge at the eastern end of the station on 12 December 1963 an ex-GWR '4700' Class thunders towards Wolverhampton on a fitted freight. The exchange sidings are well populated with 'Prairie' and 'Pannier' tank locomotives both positioned at the head of eastbound freights. Note the spur leading to the goods bay platform on the left.

Looking east from Wednesbury Great Western Street tram stop on 7 November 2009, tram No 11 whisks its way towards West Bromwich and ultimately Birmingham Snow Hill. Of note is the parapet of the bridge just ahead of the tram, which is the very same as that immediately to the left of the steam-hauled freight in the earlier scene. How times have changed! *Peter Shoesmith/JW*

# Introduction

Staffordshire offers great diversity, ranging from the bleak moorlands in the north and the rolling hills of Cannock Chase in the central area to the generally flat lowlands of the south. The industry and commerce of the county reflects this diversity, too, with a world-renowned pottery industry in the north, agriculture and forestry across the middle of the county, and the south dominated by heavy industry and manufacturing.

That is how it was, but the world moves on, and in so doing the importance of many of the industries is now greatly diluted. It is against the background of a changing economic and industrial scene that this volume is set. It covers the southern and eastern areas of the county and is intended to complement both our earlier volume, No 61, Birmingham, and Hugh Ballantyne's No 50, North Staffordshire.

In contrast to the north of the county, the geography of the south is much less spectacular, with the rolling and forested hills of Cannock Chase the most notable feature. To the north of 'The Chase', as it is known locally, runs the Trent Valley, through which the infant river meanders through meadow and flood plain across the central belt and eastern flank of the county on its way to join forces with the River Ouse prior to flowing into the North Sea.

Apart from Cannock Chase, the south and east of the county is not known for its natural beauty. Instead, it is generally thought of as the 'Black Country', the heavily industrialised area that was once in the vanguard of the Industrial Revolution. So termed in 1862 as 'black by day, and red by night', it presented a forest of chimney stacks belching out smoke in the daytime while the night sky was lit up with the fires of the iron and steel works. At its zenith it was estimated that there were more than 100 blast furnaces operating within the Black Country at any one time. The origin of the term is obscure, as there is a general belief that it was coined to describe the black soot from the chimneys that blanketed the area. However, there is evidence that the term actually pre-dates industrialisation, and refers to the black soil common to the area, which was due to contamination from the shallow coal seams on which the Black Country's future prosperity was to be based.

To attempt to define the area is almost impossible, as even local opinions vary, often vociferously. It has no official boundary, although the Ordnance Survey has just recently acknowledged the name for future mapping purposes. Perhaps the nearest historical definition is based on the '30 foot seam' of coal that encompasses such famous names as West Bromwich, Cradley Heath, Old Hill, Blackheath, Tipton, Bilston and Wednesbury. It should be noted that, although commonly connected to the Black Country, Wolverhampton and Walsall are not regarded as being members of that exclusive club!

On the back of iron and steel production grew a multiplicity of associated industries and trades, resulting in the rapid expansion of the area and the prosperity enjoyed within the West Midlands conurbation for many years. The range of products was staggering, from the miniscule to the mighty, from basic to intricate. Nails and screws were produced alongside locks and fasteners, while motor cars and precision machine tools contrasted with anchors and chains for ships, the most famous example of the latter being those for the ill-fated RMS Titanic.

Competition from foreign markets and economic recessions at home eventually took their toll, and to drive around the region today, as we have done for the 'present' photographs, is a depressing experience, with derelict industrial premises, usually devoid of their roofs or with all windows boarded up, an all too common sight. Many have not survived at all, and much of what seems to be waste ground was once occupied by manufacturing. Although the area has suffered economically, the skill-base and diversity of trades has meant that the Black Country is still predominantly industrial, although at a scale much reduced from its heyday.

The diversity of the region is not shared by what was once the Cannock Chase coalfield. Situated to the north of the '30 foot seam' that defined the South Staffordshire coalfield, it was located mainly to the east and north of Cannock and in its heyday was a very productive area, served by a significant number of pits. Over the years these have gradually closed, although the last, Littleton, survived until 1993 when its closure was somewhat tarnished by the undue haste with which the event was executed. There was no fallback to other industries or trades, and the area has struggled economically since.

North east of Cannock Chase is Burton-upon-Trent, the brewery capital of the UK. Located at a key point on the River Trent, the brewery industry here dates back to the late 17th century when the waters of the Trent were first put to good use. Even then, despite the poor transport links of the time, quantities of beer were being appreciated in the capital, which was to be a precursor of the huge quantities that were to flow a couple of centuries later.

The early 19th century witnessed tremendous change, but the catalyst that enabled the new industries of the Black Country, Cannock Chase and Burton-upon-Trent to prosper was improved transport, that vital ability to import raw materials efficiently then export finished goods to market quickly. The growth of the canal network is the late 18th and early 19th centuries had already made an impact, especially in the transportation of the basic raw materials of iron and steel production, coal and limestone. But it was the advent of the railways that had the seismic effect, when delivery times changed from days to hours virtually overnight.

The Grand Junction provided the first railway into Staffordshire with its route from Liverpool and Manchester to Birmingham. It managed to bypass Wolverhampton and Walsall in so doing, as Birmingham and a connection with the London & Birmingham was the objective, which effectively opened up a main line from the North West to London. Walsall actually beat Wolverhampton onto the railway map when the South Staffordshire opened its line from the town to Bescot in 1847, some five years before the London & North Western Railway, the product of a now merged London & Birmingham and Grand Junction, reached Wolverhampton (High Level) by way of the Stour Valley route.

The Great Western was not sitting back either, as it had designs on both the local coalfields and extending its broad gauge tracks to Liverpool, it reached Wolverhampton (Low Level) in 1854 from Birmingham Snow Hill, and Dudley two years after the LNWR. The combined Birmingham and Dudley routes also created a little Black Country network for the Great Western. The GWR also joined up with the Shrewsbury & Birmingham Railway, the latter having effectively lost a protracted battle with the LNWR for running rights over the Stour Valley line to Birmingham New Street. The die was now cast – both the LNWR and the GWR had through routes to London, but the latter's ambition to extend the broad gauge to Liverpool was thwarted by Parliament, which insisted that standard gauge should prevail throughout, and Wolverhampton remained the northern outpost of the wider gauge.

The LNWR also got its hands on the South Staffordshire line, a strategically important route from Wichnor Junction, on the Midland's Birmingham to Derby main line, which ran via Walsall to Dudley and onwards to the Great Western line to Stourbridge and beyond (the old Oxford, Worcester & Wolverhampton route). Meanwhile, the Midland had consolidated its territory from Derby with the main line to Birmingham and Bristol, but had little presence in the Black Country, with only a line from Castle Bromwich to Wolverhampton via Willenhall and Wednesfield, with access to Walsall via Ryecroft Junction. Walsall was, and is, the key in that the Wolverhampton route always struggled while the easterly section, which runs through Sutton Park to Walsall, remains today an important freight route.

Amid all the jostling for position, perhaps the most strategic route in Staffordshire was promoted and built without a hitch. This was the Trent Valley line from Rugby to Stafford via Tamworth and Lichfield, which opened in 1847 and bypassed the already congested West Midlands with traffic from London to the North West and onwards to Scotland. The route remains today one of the busiest and most varied for motive power, and whose importance was recognised by a multi-million-pound investment in quadrupling the

BURTON-UPON-TRENT: In the 'brewery capital of the UK', looking west from the footbridge that spanned the maze of running lines of the Shobnall branch, 'Jinty' 0-6-0T No 47643 is seen shunting the sidings to Bass's New Ales Stores, behind which is the chimney of its cask washing plant. To the left is the curve to Bass's Shobnall Maltings. Sandwiched between the two sets of sidings is Shobnall Crossing signal box, next to which is an unusual cross-bar signal. To the right of the 'Jinty' is Shobnall Exchange Sidings, and on the extreme right the single-line branch to Marston's Brewery.

The Shobnall branch was the last of the brewery systems to close in October 1979. The footbridge from which the previous photograph was taken has also been removed, so today we have a different viewpoint to the right from Shobnall Road, which runs parallel to where the branch was located. By necessity the viewpoint is also further forward, but Marston's Brewery on the right clearly identifies the location. A basin off the Trent & Mersey Canal has been extended into where the exchange sidings once stood, and a new industrial unit also occupies roughly the same spot. *Phil Waterfield/ GD*

tracks between Tamworth and Armitage as part of the overall West Coast upgrade ahead of the introduction of 125mph Virgin 'Pendolino' services in 2005.

What of the future? The Midland Metro tramway is looking to expand, and an evaluation of 'tram-train' technology could see the proposed extension from Wednesbury to the Merry Hill Shopping Centre via Dudley continue via the 'heavy rail' tracks to also serve Stourbridge. Additionally, there is a proposal for a completely 'light rail' loop around Wolverhampton city centre concentrating on a new rail, bus and tram interchange close to Wolverhampton High Level station.

On the national network the reopening of the northern section of the South Staffordshire route between Ryecroft Junction and Lichfield is also being proposed, although it is unlikely that anything will happen until well into the next decade. The growing importance of the National Arboretum at Alrewas could well act as a catalyst for reopening of the local station, which would then only involve a short walk to the centre, and for operating convenience, involve the extension of any new service from Lichfield via Alrewas and Wichnor Junction to Burton-upon-Trent. The route is also seen as a potential freight bypass for Birmingham.

We hope that you will share with us the enjoyment of a photographic excursion around this diverse region. It is not intended to be a definitive historical document or photographic record , but will hopefully provide a flavour of the south and east of Staffordshire in the past, and what it has to offer in the future. Maybe the demise of the industrialised Black Country casts a shadow, as represented by the run-down parts of that region, but overall the signs are of regeneration. New industries are being developed, together with new skills. The transport infrastructure has been greatly enhanced and, as mentioned earlier, there are a number of exciting projects in the pipeline. Even the canals, written off in the 1960s, are now being restored and used for recreational purposes as well as providing potential commercial opportunities.

Compiling this book has meant revisiting places from our childhood, places we had not been to for decades. It rekindled many happy memories that enhanced the fun and enjoyment of collating the entire project. Our grateful thanks go to all the people who have proactively helped us with this book, either by providing access to their photographic collections, advising on captioning information or helping to pinpoint particular locations. To all, we are indebted.

**John Whitehouse**
**Geoff Dowling**

# BIBLIOGRAPHY

Boyton, John
    **Rails Around Walsall**
    **Main Line to Metro** (Birmingham Snow Hill-Wolverhampton)
    (Both: Mid England Books)
Christiansen, Rex
    **A Regional History of the Railways of Great Britain: Vol 7 The West Midlands**
    **Forgotten Railways: Vol 10 The West Midlands**
    (Both: David & Charles)
Collins, Paul
    **Rail Centres: Wolverhampton**
    (Ian Allan)
Docherty, Andrew
    'Rail Around Birmingham', internet website
    **Rail Around Birmingham: Central Birmingham**
    **Rail Around Birmingham: The Black Country and South Staffordshire**
    (Both: Silver Link Publishing)
Pixton, Bob
    **Birmingham-Derby: Portrait of a Famous Route**
    (Runpast Publishing)
Shepherd, Cliff
    **Brewery Railways of Burton on Trent**
    (Industrial Railway Society)
Shill, R. M.
    **Industrial Locomotives of South Staffordshire**
    (Industrial Railway Society)
Twells, H. N.
    **The Railways in and around Burton-upon-Trent**
    (Booklaw/Railbus Publications)
Williams, Ned
    **Railways of the Black Country Vols 1 & 2**
    (Uralia Press)

# Grand Junction
# north of Wolverhampton

PENKRIDGE: The first main-line route to enter Staffordshire was the Grand Junction Railway, and south of Stafford the village of Penkridge became the first of three rural halts preceding Wolverhampton. Penkridge, unlike the other two, Gailey and Four Ashes, is the only one to survive through to the present day. It owes its existence to Baron Hatherton, a landowner of some influence whose enduring agreement that the Grand Junction could cross his land was conditional on the GJR providing a station at Penkridge. The station itself is perched on an embankment on the western edge of the village and is served by local trains only. Distinctive whitewashed booking hall and waiting rooms feature on the up platform, but are on this occasion obscured by the presence of Fairburn 2-6-4T No 42603 on a short parcels train. Note the extended wooden platform beyond the train.

British Railways tried to close Penkridge in 1962 together with the other intermediate stations between Stafford and Wolverhampton, but were thwarted by the present Baron Hatherton, who threatened to withdraw the consent given by his predecessor for the railway to cross the family's land. So a quirk of history ensures that Penkridge, which remains essentially a village despite the significant growth in housing over recent years, retains its station when much larger towns remain bereft of such a facility. The station has recently been modernised, resulting in the loss of the footbridge and with access to Platform 2 now by way of a subway at the Wolverhampton end, together with a lengthy wheelchair-friendly ramp. The whitewashed station booking office and waiting room remain on Platform 1, albeit now boarded up. On 19 November Class 221 'Voyager' No 221128 hurries south with a Cross-Country working to Bournemouth.
*John Bucknall/JW*

LITTLETON BRANCH: The branch from Penkridge to Littleton Colliery was roughly 2½ miles in length and, after curving around the southern boundary of the village, pass beneath the M6 motorway then crossed the Staffordshire & Worcestershire Canal, it headed virtually in a straight line towards Huntingdon, where the mine was located. The line was built on the course of a horse-drawn tramway to the canal at Otherton on the outskirts of Penkridge, and opened as a standard gauge railway in 1901. The branch was diesel-hauled for around the last 20 years of its life, and trains were handled by powerful 750hp General Electric Traction 0-6-0 locomotives, one of which is seen drawing a rake of loaded HAA 'merry-go-round' wagons for the BR exchange sidings across a minor road near Otherton, just before the line passes beneath the M6. Note the British Telecom relay tower at Pye Green to the left of the locomotive.

Littleton Colliery became the last surviving pit of the Cannock Chase coalfield and was closed, quite abruptly, at the end of 1993. The branch closed with it, and was soon lifted. Its course is still easy to follow and even the crossing gates protecting the level crossing over the minor road near Otherton survive. Although a hazy day, the BT Relay Tower is just visible on the horizon. *Both JW*

# Wolverhampton and LMS routes

WOLVERHAMPTON HIGH LEVEL: By the mid-19th century Wolverhampton was already important in its own right, although it has always tended to be overshadowed by its major competitor and neighbour, Birmingham. At the dawn of the railway age the town became a battleground when the ambitions of Euston and Paddington collided head-on. The LNWR reached the town first, and High Level station (originally known as Queen Street) was established in 1852. This happened against the acrimonious background of the LNWR intention of frustrating the attempts by the Shrewsbury & Birmingham (S&B) gaining access to its Stour Valley route and into New Street station. The LNWR won, and the S&B amalgamated with the GWR two years later. Not only did it win the war with the S&B, but the LNWR retained the physical high ground with its High Level station. However its competitors did not achieve all their ambitions, particularly the GWR, whose plan to extend the broad gauge to Merseyside hit the buffers at Wolverhampton. The fact that High level survives today gives a clear indication as to who won the railway battle of Wolverhampton. With electrification looming, the station, and its typical LNWR-style all-over roof, is on borrowed time before redevelopment, as 'Britannia' No 70031 *Byron* draws to a stop with a Birmingham New Street to Manchester Piccadilly service.

High Level was one of many stations rebuilt to meet the dawn of the new 'electric' age, and as such is typical of the minimalistic, uncomplicated architecture of the day. Although criticised today for lack of style, it is a good representative of its age. Finished in 1967, it remains today virtually unaltered except for a new platform and the construction of a rather incongruous new footbridge at the northern end in conjunction with the new Platform 4. However, a further rebuild is in the wind, as part of a major transport interchange with buses and the Metro. Plans are at an advanced stage, and no doubt the new footbridge will blend more easily into the next regeneration of High Level. The new age of traction is illustrated on 23 November 2009 as recently introduced Class 350 EMU No 350106 heads north with the 11.36 semi-fast service from Birmingham New Street to Liverpool. *Brian Robbins/JW*

*Right* **WOLVERHAMPTON HIGH LEVEL's** train shed was of classic LNWR design, but due to the restricted elevated site it was rather narrow and tended to be gloomy. The overall roof survived until February 1965 when it was demolished as part of the rebuilding of the station for the 'electric age'. In fact, the roof was quite an attractive feature, especially when compared with the 'minimalistic' design that followed. There is a wealth of interest on Platform 1, ranging from the typical Wymans stall for newspapers and magazines to the piles of parcels at the far end, awaiting despatch. The date is 28 September 1963, which was a Saturday, and considering it is just past 12.15pm the station looks remarkably quiet. *Roger Shenton*

*Above* **WOLVERHAMPTON HIGH LEVEL:** Southbound trains leaving High Level were immediately faced with a tight reverse curve on the approach to Crane Street Junction, which is where the Midland route to Walsall diverged from the LNWR Stour Valley line to Birmingham. At nearby Heath Town a spur from the Midland line connected to the Grand Junction at Portobello Junction to complete the 'Wolverhampton Loop', which enabled trains using that company's line to gain access to the town. Looking back into High Level station, the old LNWR roof can be seen as rebuilt 'Royal Scot' 4-6-0 No 46169 *The Boy Scout* eases a southbound express from Platform 2. On the extreme right is a glimpse of the clock tower on the roof of the Springfield Brewery, emphasising the curvature of the LNWR route through Wolverhampton.

14

The southbound exit remains restricted due to the tight track curvature, and beyond Crane Street Junction the Stour Valley route then continues along a low viaduct for several hundred yards before the terrain levels. Therefore any future easing of the curves to increase line speed would be a very costly affair. Looking back into the station on 23 November 2009, Virgin 'Pendolino' No 390035 *City of Lancaster* is laying over in Platform 2 prior to forming the 1245 service to London Euston. On the left is the south-end bay platform, behind which is the now redundant parcels dock. The new Platform 4 can be seen on the right, while the remains of Springfield Brewery are hidden behind the new apartment tower, which occupies the trackbed of the Great Western line. *John Bucknall/ JW*

WOLVERHAMPTON HIGH LEVEL: Looking towards Crane Street Junction from the north end of Platform 3 on 26 August 1978, Class 86 No 86012 takes the through road with an ECS working from the nearby Oxley carriage sidings to Birmingham New Street. Behind the train are three running lines; these are actually sidings, which at the time were primarily used for stabling locomotives. Another facet of the railway at this time was the 'BRUTE' (British Railways Utility Trolley Equipment) loaded with parcels awaiting the next Euston service. 'Red Star', BR's own parcels service, used passenger trains of the day to convey goods and the BRUTES were the means of carriage of the parcels to and from the trains, and, indeed, on the trains. Just ahead of the locomotive can be seen the flat-roofed power signal box, behind which is the old ex-LNWR Mill Street Goods Station.

The provision of a new Platform 4 on the eastern side of High Level together with the new footbridge at the northern end were the first major additions to the station since it was rebuilt as part of the LMR West Coast Electrification Scheme. The design of platform contrasts with more than complements the remainder of the station as its curved roof varies from the straight lines and right-angles typified by the older buildings. Still, its reflective qualities are well illustrated as Class 350 No 350130's departure working the 1034 Liverpool Lime Street to Birmingham New Street semi-fast service on 23 November 2009 is mirrored in the glazed panelling of the new platform. Note the gabled end of the long-closed Mill Street Goods Depot, which is now part of an inner-city redevelopment project. *Both JW*

COSELEY: The original Coseley & Deepfields station opened in 1852, and was replaced in 1902 by a new station a short distance away, which dropped the 'Deepfields' part of the title. It is now the first station south of Wolverhampton on the busy Stour Valley route following the closure of Ettingshall Road in 1964 and Monmore Green even earlier in 1916. This September 1966 view shows Coseley at the dawn of the 'electric age' with a Metro-Cammell Class 101 DMU calling with a Birmingham New Street service. The station had yet to lose its canopy on the up side and the whole appearance reeks of neglect. Maybe BR should have noted the advert for Snowcem masonry paint, as a touch of whitewash would certainly have brightened up the place!

The station was rationalised post-electrification, and the buildings and canopy on the up side removed completely, being replaced for several years by what can best be described as a booking hut and a bus-stop waiting shelter. It is good to note that the station has now been modernised, and a new booking hall, constructed at road level, together with a new platform waiting room have been provided on the up side. The gem though is the retention of the original waiting room and its canopy, which survived electrification and now offers a different atmosphere to passengers in contrast with the new buildings. Compared with the neglect of 1966, the station is now a credit to the system. On 12 December 2009 Class 350 No 350238 calls with a Liverpool Lime Street to Birmingham New Street service. *Peter Shoesmith/GD*

DUDLEY PORT was considered by the LNWR to be a key location, not so much due to its presence on the Stour Valley main line, but due to its ability to serve nearby Dudley by way of a half-mile chord that ran from the main line just to the north of the station to the South Staffordshire line and thence to Dudley. It was for a time the country's most intensive local service, with 70 return trips each weekday. The spur also enabled the LNWR to route through trains from Euston to Dudley. This view, taken on 27 July 1964, is looking along the Birmingham Canal, and the bridge carrying the spur to Dudley over the waterway can be seen in the background, to the right of which is the signal box, which closed in August 1965 when the area was transferred to Wolverhampton power signal Box. A Fowler Class 4F can be seen at the head a short rake of wagons. The absence of signals on the gantry indicates that the Dudley shuttle service has recently been withdrawn. The location of the Low Level line can be determined by the bridge seen in the foreground.

Dudley Port station today remains hidden behind the brick wall and wooden fence, with just the colour light signal and overhead electrification masts betraying the presence of the railway. Added arboreal growth over recent years adds further camouflage to the national network. The abutments of the bridge that carries the canal over the Low Level line from Dudley to Walsall can just be seen where the canal narrows, and further along, roughly where the pipe is carried over the canal, is where the branch from Dudley Port to Dudley diverged from the main line and crossed the canal. The branch was well known for its connection with Palethorpe's Sausages, whose products were exported by rail from sidings just north of Dudley Port in company-liveried vans. *Roger Shenton/GD*

SANDWELL & DUDLEY station started life as Oldbury in 1852 with the opening of the Stour Valley line. It is situated on an embankment, a little more than a mile from West Bromwich town centre, making it the closest LNWR competitor to the GWR's centrally located station. The construction was typical of the line with wooden platforms and station buildings, and this September 1966 scene shows the station with its canopies removed to accommodate the electrification of the line. The absence of the canopies reveals their attractive wrought-iron supports as well as the typical LNWR station design. A Metro-Cammell Class 101 DMU is seen departing with a Birmingham New Street to Wolverhampton High Level local service.

The station received a boost when the GWR main line finally closed in 1972, and its future was secured when in 1983 it was completely rebuilt and renamed Sandwell & Dudley in recognition of the much wider catchment area it now served. Originally designated a 'Parkway', it offers good parking facilities and is now the principal intermediate station between Wolverhampton and New Street. Of significance, the station's services were greatly enhanced with long-distance trains now calling, particularly direct Virgin services to London Euston. On 12 December 2009 Class 323 No 323210 departs with the 1039 New Street to Wolverhampton all-stations stopping service. Each platform now has platform waiting rooms, while the booking hall is located at street level on the up side. *Peter Shoesmith/GD*

SPON LANE station opened with LNWR's Stour Valley line in 1852 and was one of a number of fringe stations serving West Bromwich, although it was actually located in the neighbouring parish of Smethwick. It catered for local traffic through to the end, as evidenced by this charming scene showing a two-car Metro-Cammell Class 101 DMU about to depart for Wolverhampton. A mother and child look to be the only passengers alighting, and appear to have just surrendered their ticket. Spon Lane signal box, beyond the bridge, is hidden behind the DMU. Notice also the distant pointwork, which connected to a goods loop running behind the station on the down side. On 17 May 1963, little more than a year before closure, the best that can be said is that the booking hall, situated on Spon Lane road bridge, is looking a little careworn, although the two waiting rooms are in better condition. Judging by the crown-type chimney pots on all three buildings, there was still an intention to stay warm despite impending closure.

Closure came in 1964, and nothing remains of the station today, with just the redundant right-hand arch of Spon Lane bridge hinting at the existence of the goods loop. Out of picture to the left are the remains of Chance's Glass Works, which is now the sorry shell of a once proud factory. The area is displaying signs of resilience with new industrial parks having been created on both sides of the railway and the canal, the latter running in a cutting beneath the Stour Valley line. The role of Spon Lane has, in time, been usurped to the north by today's Sandwell & Dudley Parkway, and more recently to the south by Smethwick Galton Bridge, opened in 1995. Passing the site of the old station on 29 November 2009 is a Virgin Class 390 'Pendolino' forming the 10.50 London Euston to Wolverhampton service. *Peter Shoesmith/JW*

DARLASTON was one of two stations on the Grand Junction route from Wolverhampton, the other being Willenhall. Together with its near neighbour Wednesbury, Darlaston was once a centre of manufacturing excellence and the home of many well-known names of British industry. The station was situated just to the north of the aptly named Darlaston Junction, where the line from Pleck Junction, Walsall, joins the main line. It was an architectural delight, with the attractive barrel-roofed wooden waiting room on the Wolverhampton-bound platform perhaps its finest feature. The booking hall, also of wood, stood on the Walsall Road, while the accommodation on the Birmingham and Walsall-bound platforms also boasted a fine canopy. Note the parcels trolley parked at the foot of the footbridge steps. A Wolverhampton-bound Class 104 DMU approaches, probably a working from Burton-upon-Trent via Walsall, is met by the expectant gaze of a couple of young trainspotters. Just visible above the DMU, beyond the road bridge, is Darlaston Junction signal box which controlled the junctions with the Darlaston Loop from Wednesbury and the line from Walsall. A station has stood on this site since 1837 and was known originally as Darlaston James Bridge until 1913 in order to differentiate it from the Darlaston station that existed on the Loop line from 1863 to 1867. Considering that this scene is less than two years before closure, the station looks to be in remarkably good condition.

Nothing remains today, any remnants having been swept away when the line was electrified shortly after closure. By necessity this is an elevated view from Kendricks Road looking down onto the station site. Note the lettering on the wall of the building on the extreme right of the 1963 shot, which remains today (although the factory has also long since closed). A London Marylebone to Wrexham service headed by a Driving Van Trailer with a DBS Class 67 propelling from the rear scurries through on 3 December *2009. Peter Shoesmith/JW*

# Bescot

BESCOT is seen in a quite amazing panorama on 15 October 1964, with the down yard area having apparently befallen some calamity judging by the barren outlook from the station footbridge. In fact, the yard is in the process of reconstruction; it will eventually become a 'hump' shunt facility, with the 'hump' to the right of Bescot No 2 signal box seen beyond the end of the down platform. The signal box had little more than 12 months to go, as it was replaced with the introduction of MAS controlled from the newly commissioned Walsall power signal box, about a mile away at Pleck Junction. The station, whose platforms are in the process of being lengthened, opened in 1847 and the goods yard in 1881 on the up side, followed by the down yard one year later.

Except for the floodlighting towers, of which one seems to have been removed, the scene today reflects a completely different railway age. Between these two images, Bescot went through the stage of 'hump'-shunting where railwaymen with long unhooking poles could be seen chasing wagons along the various reception sidings to the clatter of buffers impacting with buffers as they collided with each other as part of the shunting process. The yard now deals with block trains, which require minimal re-marshalling. The reception sidings display a range of wagons, including Network Rail infrastructure stock. A 'virtual quarry' has been created on the left, and a rake of engineer's wagons can be seen in the course of being loaded. The new station booking hall and waiting room occupy Platform 1, while Class 323 No 323216 approaches with the late-running 1219 Wolverhampton to Walsall service via Birmingham New Street on 14 November 2009. *Roger Shenton/JW*

BESCOT's current station predates the goods yard by 34 years, although the Grand Junction had earlier opened a station nearby in 1837 to cater for the then expanding town of Walsall, which it had inconveniently avoided when planning the original route into Birmingham. The South Staffordshire's connection to Walsall opened in 1847, for which the new station was constructed. Although strategically positioned, Bescot's role was always freight, with passenger business being mainly commuter-based, as the Stour Valley route had captured most of the long-distance passenger traffic. A typical freight approaches the station from the Walsall line hauled by ex-LNWR Bowen-Cooke 'G2' Class 7F 0 8 0 No 49406 running tender-first. The driver looks to be peering over the well-stocked tender, no doubt to check that he has favourable signals ahead. On the down platform an engineman strides purposefully to work with tea-can in hand. Electrification and redevelopment of the yard in the 1960s were to change this scene completely.

An all-new station awaits the visitor today, following a rebuild of the basic 1960s-style structure that replaced the LNWR station seen in the earlier scene. The footbridge is now of pre-cast concrete, while the booking hall has an impressive gabled roof. Only a 'bus-stop'-style shelter is available on the northbound platform. The colour light signal protects Bescot Junction, with the 'feather' governing access to the Walsall line. DBS Class 67 No 67012 *A Shropshire Lad* heads a Wrexham to London Marylebone service through the station on 26 November 2009. *Eric Rogers/JW*

23

BESCOT: Looking towards Wolverhampton from Bescot station footbridge in the early 1950s we see an unrebuilt 'Royal Scot' approaching with a diverted express. Such diversions are common up to the present day, during closure of the Trent Valley route for engineering work. The South Staffordshire line to Walsall diverges on the right, while the express is approaching on the original Grand Junction route from the north. Running behind the signal box is the line from the goods yard, which splits to join the Grand Junction at a point above the first coach of the train, as well as crossing the Grand Junction on the flat to reach the South Staffs line to Walsall, or to Wednesbury via Bescot Curve Junction. On the extreme left there is a glimpse of Bescot shed tucked away behind the signal box. Note also the well-kept hedge within the confines of what appears to be a mess-room on the right-hand side.

The basic layout of Bescot Junction has altered little over the years, as can be seen in this view of 14 November 2009 with DBS Class 67 No 67012 *A Shropshire Lad* approaching from Wolverhampton with a Wrexham to London Marylebone service. It does not stop at Bescot, but picks up at Tame Bridge Parkway, a recently opened station little more than a mile further on, which boasts superior car parking facilities. On the left is DBS Class 60 No 60022, which still carries the livery of freight operator English, Welsh & Scottish Railways; it had recently been acquired by DB, the German State railway operator, which now operates the company under the title of DB Schenker (DBS). In the background can be seen the remains of the old Bescot steam shed. *Eric Rogers/JW*

BESCOT: Looking back towards Bescot Junction from the footbridge on the Grand Junction route, some shunting seems to be taking place. The station and signal box can be seen in the background while an unidentified Class 7F 0-8-0 faces Wolverhampton and a 'Black 5' and another 7F are tender-to-tender on the spur from the yard. The rear wall of the motive power depot is on the right, in front of which are a couple of wagons on the private siding belonging to well-known garden tool manufacturer Spear & Jackson. A stream flows behind the depot and beneath the railway to join the River Tame which flows next to the railway on the left. At this time the river was quite a noxious waterway because of the high level of pollution caused by local industries discharging their waste into it.

The overhead electrification masts dominate the scene today, but the trackwork has not altered that much in the intervening years, except for the loss of the siding into Spear & Jackson's works, which, like most of its neighbours, has long since closed. The rear wall of the old steam shed still stands, while the new interloper on the left is the elevated section of the M6 motorway. Driving Van Trailer No 82304 heads a London Marylebone to Shrewsbury service on 20 November 2009, its traction being a DBS Class 67 propelling from the rear. *R. Selvey collection/JW*

BESCOT: Looking towards Wolverhampton from the same Grand Junction footbridge presents a different scene with Bowen Cooke 'G2' Class 7F 0-8-0 No 49430 running towards Bescot tender-first with a short freight. This scene dates from the mid-1960s, yet the locomotive's tender still bears the marks where the 'LMS' lettering once appeared, and its cabside carries the distinctive yellow stripe indicating that the locomotive is banned from operating under the electrified wires due to restricted clearances. The allotments are enclosed by the chord from Bescot to Wednesbury at Bescot Curve Junction, this line can be seen passing over the Grand Junction route on the distant overbridge. The locomotive is just passing over the River Tame, which skirts the length of Bescot Yard.

The scene today is dominated by the M6 motorway, which is carried across the flood plain of the River Tame on a lengthy viaduct around a mile long. Junction 9 for Wednesbury and Walsall is signposted in the background; this is one of the busiest stretches of road in Europe and the constant thunder of the traffic is inescapable. Wrexham & Shropshire-liveried DBS Class 67 No 67012 *A Shropshire Lad* heads a Wrexham to London Marylebone service on 20 November 2009. *R. Selvey collection/JW*

**TAME BRIDGE PARKWAY:** Looking down from the commanding position of the aqueduct that carries the Tame Valley Canal over the Grand Junction provided a good perspective on the Bescot area in the 1950s. In the background is the old Walsall Road bridge, at the neck of Bescot Yard, and ahead of the bridge are the two loops giving access to it. On the right-hand side can be seen a short rake of wagons standing on a spur that was laid into an underground munitions factory situated to the right of the River Tame. Heading south at the point where Tame Bridge Parkway station is now located is a diverted up express hauled by rebuilt 'Jubilee' No 45736 *Phoenix*. This was one of two 'Jubilees' rebuilt with a larger boiler, double chimney and smoke deflectors, thus acquiring a higher power rating of 7P.

Of many significant changes, the most important is the provision of a new station called Tame Bridge Parkway, which opened in 1990. The provision of a large car park and a location more convenient than nearby Bescot has made the new station a great success. Charter operators have more recently identified its worth and the station now features regularly as a pick-up point for railtours. The old Walsall Road has been replaced by a dual carriageway which crosses the railway on a new bridge, while the old bridge is now only used for access to Bescot Yard. In the background, surrounded by Bescot's floodlights, is the sloping-roofed building that is the RAC Traffic Control Centre situated next to the M6. The station is occupied by Class 323s Nos 323220 and 323218 (right), operating Birmingham New Street to Walsall stopping services on 20 November 2009. *R. Selvey collection/JW*

# Walsall

Walsall was an important railway centre, perhaps more so than has ever been properly acknowledged, as in 1900 it was recording around 1,000 train movements a day. The town was initially overlooked by the Grand Junction, which sited its 'Walsall' station close to the site of the present Bescot Stadium station, with a horse-drawn coach connection only. A branch to Walsall had been approved by the Act of Parliament that authorised the Grand Junction Railway, but it was never built.

Walsall joined the railway age in 1849 when the South Staffordshire set up its headquarters in the town, which in turn became the principal station on the company's new route from Wichnor Junction to Dudley. The South Staffordshire was eventually absorbed by the LNWR after a period of 'joint stewardship' with the Midland Railway. The Midland, also, was active and was responsible for a new line from Water Orton to Wolverhampton. The town became a central point for local passenger traffic with direct trains to Wolverhampton, Dudley, Birmingham New Street via both Perry Barr and Sutton Coldfield, together with Lichfield and Burton-upon-Trent.

PLECK JUNCTION: A pair of Class 20s are signal-checked on the approach to Pleck Junction, where three routes diverge. The actual junction is a short distance away in the direction of Walsall, and the lines seen in this February 1991 view are, on the extreme left, from Walsall to Bescot, and the South Staffordshire route from Wednesbury, over which the freight has just travelled. By this time the South Staffordshire line was in its final throes, as complete closure between Walsall and Brierley Hill was just two years away.

The layout today remains unchanged except for the South Staffordshire line being gradually reclaimed by nature. Notice that the signal, at which the Class 20s were halted in the earlier picture, remains, but the route has been fenced off. On the left, approaching from Bescot, is Class 153 No 153354 leading a Class 170 DMU on the 10.39 Birmingham New Street to Rugeley Trent Valley service on 30 November 2009. Plans remain to reopen the line at some stage, in part with a scheme to extend the Midland Metro tram system from Wednesbury to Dudley by utilising a portion of the trackbed. *Both JW*

PLECK JUNCTION is where the quadruple running lines southbound from Walsall diverge. Heading off to the right is the spur to Darlaston Junction on the Wolverhampton line, while straight ahead is for Bescot and the South Staffordshire line to Dudley; the crossovers for these two lines are out of picture on the right. In the summer of 1965 Class 9F 2-10-0 No 92063 is seen running from Walsall to Bescot, while the right-hand pair of tracks are to and from Dudley. This scene is pre-electrification and shows the old Pleck Junction LNWR-pattern signal box. Of note is that Walsall power signal box is in an advanced stage of construction and will soon take over the signalling function for the area.

The complex overhead wiring layout has to mirror the various running line options at Pleck Junction today, which makes for a much more cluttered scene. The basic layout remain, though, with the power signal box on the left, the quadruple running lines and the chord to Darlaston Junction diverging on the right. Class 153 No 153365 and a Class 170 DMU form the 14.39 Birmingham New Street to Rugeley Trent Valley service on 23 November 2009, and have just negotiated the crossover from the Bescot route in order to gain access to Walsall's Platform 1.
*R. Selvey collection/JW*

WALSALL: A further reminder of the extent of the railway infrastructure at Walsall is well illustrated in this early 1960s view looking from Corporation Street towards Pleck Junction. On the right is a fan of sidings dealing with freight traffic, while further in the background is the bulk of Walsall Gas Works, with its coal conveyor belt on the extreme right. On the left are sidings for storing the coaching stock that would be called upon to cover relief and excursion traffic. A 'Black 5' No 44829 heads for Walsall on what looks to be a weekend excursion train.

A slightly wider view today reveals that the carriage sidings have long been ripped up, and more recently replaced by a cement terminal which is fed by rail from the Peak District. On 26 November 2009 the wagons are in the process of being discharged as train engine, DBS Class 66 No. 66121, is ready to back onto the rake for the return working. The four track formation remains, but little else. The area where the gas works sidings stood is now waste land, and the introduction of natural gas rendered the gas works redundant a few decades ago. *R. Selvey collection/JW*

WALSALL: This view is from the surviving island platform looking back at the 1923-vintage booking hall, and shows well what a fine-looking building it was. It is said that the splendidly rebuilt new station was a parting gesture of thanks to Walsall from the LNWR for the prosperity the town had generated for the railway company who had been the custodian of the station since the absorbtion of the South Staffordshire Railway. By the time it was finished and formally opened, the LNWR itself had become part of the LMS. The booking hall stood on a raft built over the running lines, as did Park Street and the adjacent buildings. In the 1960s a further raft was built on which Littlewoods department store was constructed, thus creating a short tunnel covering the northern exit from the station. The flooding was not a one-off affair either, as up until the 1970s it was a regular occurrence, it took a multi-million-pound drainage scheme involving a series of subterranean reservoirs to resolve.

The shopping centre not only took over the station site but also extended further over the railway, the new booking office is located directly above Class 323 No 323206, which will shortly proceed with the 12.01 service to Birmingham New Street on 8 December 2009. To the left is a new walkway from the shopping centre to the platforms, which has given the station a modern appearance, although the fact that the most of the Class 323 is submerged in the gloom beneath the shopping centre does present a claustrophobic atmosphere for passengers. *R. Selvey collection/JW*

WALSALL: Amidst the many local services one long-distance express was a notable visitor to Walsall, the Manchester to Bournemouth 'Pines Express', a train probably more commonly associated with the Somerset & Dorset route. 'The Pines' changed engines at Walsall, which this photograph records, with 'Jubilee' No 45662 *Kempenfelt*, its safety valve impatiently blowing off, looking as though it is ready to come off the train to be replaced by a sister engine already waiting on the centre road. The view is from Platform 2 looking over to Platform 1 with the footbridge spanning the scene. Behind are properties situated on Station Street, and just beyond the footbridge can be seen the chimneys on top of the old South Staffordshire station building.

The South Staffordshire Railway had built their impressive head office and booking hall in 1849. Over the years it saw a number of uses, the main one being for the railway's parcels business. The steel girder seems far too extravagant to be a signal gantry and looks suspiciously like part of the footbridge that once stood in virtually the same spot. Heading north on a van train is Class 44 No 44004 on 26 September 1977. Note that by this time the locomotive's *Great Gable* nameplate had been removed by BR as part of a policy of de-naming diesel locomotives.

The view looking towards Bescot nowadays offers a complete contrast. All the buildings on the far side have been demolished and the new 'Saddlers' shopping centre now encroaches over the railway, so the position where the previous two photographs were taken is now beneath the new extension. Approaching is Class 170 No 170635 together with a Class 153 unit forming the 11.39 Birmingham New Street to Rugeley service on 10 December 2009. The BOAK building with its chimney on the right is a Grade 2 listed building, once engaged in the leather trade, and provides a reminder of old Walsall.
*R. Selvey Collection/JW (2)*

32

WALSALL's importance as a railway centre is graphically confirmed by this view looking across at the impressive South Staffordshire head office building and Platform 1 on 26 March 1964. The building dates back to 1849, and served as the main station building until 1871, when a new facade and booking hall was constructed to face Park Street. Looking along the platform there is a wealth of detail including contemporary railway advertising, a cycle and moped left standing against the wall without any security locks (well, this is 1964), a sign for the telegrams office, and a huge pile of parcels and what look like mailbags – all part of the railway scene in those days!

This 1977 view, again looking across from Platform 2, shows more of the detail in the imposing facade of the SSR building. Unfortunately the roof line is spoiled by a modern office block, but the sheer elegance of the building remains some 128 years after construction. The circular station booking hall can be seen in the background, behind which is the slab brick wall of the Littlewoods store, which was constructed over the railway in the early 1960s. The 'Gentlemen' sign clearly defines the purpose of the wooden slatted building on the immediate right, behind which is a more recently built railwaymen's mess-room and office. Trundling towards Bescot is a Class 45 'Peak' with just a guard's van in tow, after most likely depositing its train at Norton Junction disposal sidings situated north of nearby Pelsall.

The 'modern' office block and the mess-rooms tie in the scene today, as the major changes in and around the station are well illustrated. The old SSR head office has gone, replaced by a 'bus-stop'-style waiting room and an administrative building, while the land behind, backing onto Station Street, is a car park. 'The Saddlers' shopping centre is shown in the background together with the corner of what is quite an impressive covered walkway to the platforms. Class 170 No 170503 prepares to depart with the 11.42 Rugeley Trent Valley to Birmingham New Street service on 8 December 2009. *Roger Shenton/JW (2)*

WALSALL: Looking north from the end of Platforms 4 and 5 reveals impatient 'Britannia' No 70004 *William Shakespeare* impatiently waiting to take over an express from the south, probably 'The Pines'. The background buildings front onto Park Street, and just to the left of No 70004's tender can be seen the tower that pinpoints Walsall Town Hall. A Class 103 Park Royal DMU is stabled in the carriage sidings next to the goods yard, which is well populated with wagons, most likely used for the conveyance of domestic coal. The presence of three chimney stacks, the centre one bearing the initials of 'H&S', indicates the close proximity of manufacturing to the town centre. By way of contrast is the chapel-like building on the extreme right, which is Walsall College of Art. Until 1958 No 70004 was one of two 'Britannias' based at Nine Elms shed in London to cover the prestigious London to Paris 'Golden Arrow' boat train, which they worked between London Victoria and Folkestone.

The modern scene is looking from the end of Platforms 2 and 3, as Platforms 4 and 5 were ripped up in the early 1970s. The nearside line running through Platform 3 is essentially a bay platform, as it terminates beneath the area occupied by the shopping centre. The far line is a through road, often carrying traffic bound for Bescot, and the area once occupied by the carriage sidings and goods yard is now buried beneath the multi-storey car park that serves 'The Saddlers'. Class 323 No 323205 is seen arriving with the 11.19 local service from Wolverhampton, which runs via Birmingham New Street. The direct Wolverhampton service, which operated via Pleck Junction and Willenhall, was withdrawn in 2008 and is now subject to one 'parliamentary' train each week as formal withdrawal proceedings have not been completed. *R. Selvey collection/JW*

WALSALL: The northbound departure from Walsall was tricky especially for heavily laden freight trains as the gradient towards Ryecroft Junction was quite adverse. The gradient post, just visible to the right of the buffer beam of Stanier 'Black 5' No 44766, indicates that it is 1 in 102. Although the town could boast many sizable industrial concerns, the prosperity of the area was equally dependant on the many small businesses that grew up on the back of their larger neighbours, as evidenced by the rather ramshackle concern on the right. By contrast the 1960s-vintage Walsall Technical College building dominates the background. From an earlier era the clock tower on the extreme left indicates the position of Walsall's central bus station. The white concrete parapet of the distant railway bridge (behind the signal gantry) will shortly become the location

of Littlewoods store, which was built on a raft over the railway cutting. The train is a Sunday excursion heading towards Ryecroft Junction in June 1962. Note the double chimney on the 'Black 5', which had been further modified with roller bearings and was the 'favourite' engine of Ryecroft shed and consequently diagrammed for most of its special traffic.

British Rail was quite proactive in utilising the space above its railway at Walsall, which started off with the Littlewoods store and was followed by a multi-storey car park on the other side of the road, which can be seen in the background of this 8 December 2009. The signal gantry roughly corresponds to that in the earlier view, while to the right is where the recently demolished Walsall Technical College stood. The track has been rationalised to double track, and passing by is Freightliner Class 66/6 No 66606 on a 'merry-go-round' coal train heading for Rugeley Power Station. *Michael Mensing/JW*

35

WALSALL: 'Digging in' is the most appropriate description of this scene from North Street bridge as Fowler Class 4 0-6-0 No 44267 has its sanders full on as it pilots a Stanier Class 8F 2-8-0 running tender-first on a coal train bound for Birchills Power Station in the early 1960s. The blast from each exhaust gives an impression of the effort being expended as the train eases up the adverse gradient towards Ryecroft Junction where it will take the chord to North Walsall Junction and onwards to the power station, which is situated little more than a mile further on the Midland line to Wolverhampton. The line is flanked by the industries that for many years provided prosperity to the town, as well as the goods for the railway to carry.

The climb to North Street today is no less severe, but obviously of little concern to Stanier 'Pacific' No 6233 *Duchess of Sutherland* as it imperiously lifts Steam Dreams' 'Cathedrals Express' towards Ryecroft Junction following a water stop at Walsall station. 'Duchesses' were banned from Walsall until the early 1960s, when pre-electrification work eased clearances on a couple of bridges in the area. Suffice to say that there are reports of a couple of 'Duchess' workings prior to the clearances being eased, which appear to have passed without any noticeable nasty scratches to their paintwork. Track rationalisation has now taken place, and Walsall has also followed the national trend in that what was once an industrial area has now become predominantly residential. Note the tower of Walsall Town Hall in the centre background. *R. Selvey collection/JW*

RYECROFT JUNCTION was a rare four-way junction, and for good measure also had an avoiding line. It is situated less than a mile north of Walsall station on a rising gradient, which made the approach difficult for heavily laden freight trains – a situation that remains today. The lines fanned out on the approach, commencing with the spur to Walsall North Junction on the Midland route from Water Orton to Wolverhampton, which also served Birchills Power Station. Next was the South Staffordshire route to Cannock and Rugeley which also connected with the Trent Valley line. Both these lines curved sharply to the west while the remaining two routes were more northerly, the first being the original South Staffordshire line to Lichfield and Wichnor Junction which ran alongside the eastern spur to the Midland's line from Water Orton, in later years it has become known as the 'Sutton Park line'. The Midland route originally ran across both the Lichfield and Rugeley lines to the north of Ryecroft Junction to provide a through route to Wolverhampton, with connections to Walsall by way of the two spurs. It was a busy place made more so by the presence of Ryecroft engine shed, situated between the South Staffordshire routes to Cannock and Lichfield. A modern BR-design signal box has replaced an earlier LNWR-pattern box and the junction had been resignalled with a gantry by the early 1960s as an unidentified Bowen-Cooke Class 7 0-8-0 lumbers towards Walsall with a rake of ballast wagons.

Ryecroft Junction today is but a shadow of its former self. Just the routes to Rugeley and Water Orton remain, although there is a long-term plan to do something with the Lichfield line. The Cannock Chase route regained its passenger service in 1989 and has continued to flourish since, while the old Midland line to Water Orton through Sutton Park remains important for freight with the possibility of reopening to passenger services at some time in the future. The course of the Lichfield line is protected and plans exist for a reopening, possibly using Tramtrain technology around ten years hence. On 19 December 2009 Class 150 No 150106 crosses from the Cannock Chase line with a Rugeley Trent Valley to Birmingham New Street service. *R. Selvey Collection/JW*

37

RYECROFT JUNCTION: Looking from the bridge at Mill Lane, just north of Ryecroft Junction, we see Class 31 No 31282 dropping down from what was Lichfield Road Junction with a Leeds to Southampton freightliner service in June 1984. To the left is the line to Brownhills and Lichfield which had closed three months earlier, already the colour light signalling has been removed. The course of the old Midland 'cut-off', which ran between Lichfield Road and North Walsall Junctions, is clearly evident, as is the bridge that carried it over the Lichfield line. The Freightliner is running down the spur that gave the Midland access to Walsall which is now the main line, better known as the 'Sutton Park line'.

The view today is much restricted due to the inevitable growth of trees since the South Staffordshire route to Lichfield closed in 1984. The Sutton Park line remains busy, albeit as a freight-only route, with the occasional excursion passenger working such as this featuring fresh-from-overhaul ex-Great Western 'Castle' Class 4-6-0 No 5029 *Nunney Castle* heading a Vintage Trains working from that company's base at Tyseley to Chester on 26 April 2008. There is no urgency from the chimney of *Nunney Castle*, as it is drifting down towards Ryecroft Junction and its booked station stop at Walsall. *Both JW*

RYECROFT JUNCTION: An unidentified Bowen-Cooke Class 7F 0-8-0 rounds the curve at Proffit Street, Walsall, while heading a coal train for nearby Birchills Power Station. It is travelling along the Midland line from Water Orton that avoided Ryecroft Junction and ran from Lichfield Road Junction to North Walsall Junction. This was an extremely useful stretch of track as it avoided costly and time-consuming reversals in Walsall. Note that the train is passing over the bridge that carried the Midland route over the Cannock Chase line. Proffit Street was part of Walsall Corporation's trolleybus network, as evidenced by the poles and wiring.

The bridge abutments have long since been removed and the roadway levelled to accommodate just a subway where the railway once ran. The course of the line can be traced by following the metalled pathway to the footbridge that now crosses the Cannock Chase line. The trolleybuses survived until 1970. *R. Selvey collection/JW*

NORTH WALSALL JUNCTION was at the westerly tip of a triangle formed by the Midland route from Water Orton to Wolverhampton. Slogging hard off the 'cut-off' from Lichfield Road Junction (at the easterly tip) is Class 'G2' 0-8-0 No 49407 with a coal train bound for Birchills Power Station. The line diverging on the right is to Ryecroft Junction and provided the important connection from Walsall and Bescot. A similar connection ran between Lichfield Road and Ryecroft Junctions.

The terraced properties in the background just visible behind the tree-lined embankment are the only connecting feature between these two views taken from the Bloxwich Road overbridge. The course of the line to Lichfield Road Junction is clearly evident, while the formation to Ryecroft Junction has merged with the vegetation on the right. *R. Selvey collection/JW*

**BIRCHILLS POWER STATION:** One of Walsall's endearing landmarks was Birchills Power Station, which dominated the skyline on the western side of the town and could be seen from many miles distant. It opened in 1949 and received coal from three sources, rail, road and canal. The railway connection was by a spur off the ex-Midland Railway's Wolverhampton and Walsall line, and the sight and sound of heavily laden coal trains slogging their way out of Walsall through Ryecroft Junction was a feature for many years. The power station was deemed inefficient and closed in 1982, remaining out of use for a further three years before demolition. It employed two Ruston & Hornsby 0-4-0 diesel shunters for internal use, one of which is seen at the head of a rake of mineral wagons in the exchange sidings that were sandwiched between the Midland's line and the power station.

The Midland route to Wolverhampton was severed in the mid-1960s by the construction of the M6 motorway which runs less than a mile to the west of this location. The stub from Ryecroft Junction remained in use for the life of the power station while the middle section to Wednesfield closed completely. The remainder of the line from Wednesfield to Wolverhampton continued in use for steel traffic until the 1980s. The land occupied by Birchills Power Station has now been taken over by a retail park and the location of the sidings is roughly in the area of the Matalan store. A new road runs alongside and to the left, (out of picture) is the course of the old Midland route. *Peter Shoesmith/JW*

# Routes from Walsall

The Black Country is a region whose boundary has defied accurate demarcation from the moment the term was first coined. Basically, it covers an area of South Staffordshire and northern Worcestershire where, in the 19th century, the production of iron and steel became the staple industry as a result of the essential natural ingredients being locally available. One definition of the title refers to the blackened land and smoke-filled skies caused by the concentration of so many blast furnaces and associated industries within such a confined geographical area. In time the Black Country also became synonymous with metal manufacturing and the remnants of the associated industries are still apparent today. The railways were to play an important role in the development of the region. Of all the towns in the Black Country, Dudley stands out as being one of the most important. Historically it was mentioned in the Domesday Book, has been dominated by a castle since the 11th century and was the site of Newcomen's first steam engine in 1712. Until the recent boundary changes it was also an enclave of Worcestershire, which was surrounded by Staffordshire.

DUDLEY's railway history is complicated, due mainly to intense completion to gain monopoly access to the town; in the end it was served by two companies, the GWR and LMS. The South Staffordshire Railway, soon to be absorbed into the LNWR, was first on the scene in 1850, followed by the Oxford, Worcester & Wolverhampton in 1853. The latter company was 'overseen' by the GWR from the start but was not absorbed until 1862. Passenger services ran to Wolverhampton Low Level, Walsall and Birmingham Snow Hill, as well as a very frequent local service to nearby Dudley Port, which also provided a connection for a through service to Euston. Withdrawal of most services came early, with the town losing all of its passenger trains by mid-1964. The station nestled in the shadow of Castle Hill, and looking down from the high overbridge that spanned the valley at this point it is seen in its final form on 13 June 1964, immediately prior to closure. On the left is the wide island platform of the Great Western whose booking hall faced onto Station Street. The footbridge connects to the LMS side, whose entrance was on Tipton Street on the right. A Birmingham RC&W Class

104 DMU awaits departure with one of the final passenger workings from the town.

From a railway perspective Dudley had all the ingredients to be a highly profitable location, a fact borne out by the scramble between the GWR and LNWR to gain exclusive access to it. The reality is that it never quite realised that potential, especially in terms of passenger services, most of which were withdrawn before the Beeching era. Even then its one major success story was the Freightliner terminal, which opened in 1967 and was an instant success becoming one of Freightliner's most profitable terminals. The fact that it lost out to one of the then poorest performing terminals at Birmingham Lawley Street, to which traffic was transferred in 1989, is perhaps typical of Dudley's less than successful experience with railways. Following the withdrawal of passenger services to

Wolverhampton Low level, the Great Western line to Priestfield Junction finally closed in 1968, which just left the freight-only South Staffordshire line. This line was gradually run down ahead of closure in 1993. One of the few regular trains in the late 1980s was a Tuesdays-only Gloucester Yard to Bescot departmental, which curiously was booked for a Class 50 locomotive, a class hitherto associated with high-speed passenger work. No 50017 *Royal Oak* is seen winding through Dudley with the lengthy return working. The now closed Freightliner terminal is on the left, with its crane still in situ.

Dudley is now one of the largest towns in the UK not directly connected to the rail network. However, there are moves afoot to include Dudley in the plan of a new Midland Metro tram line, utilising the route of the now closed freight line from Wednesbury, continuing to Merry Hill Shopping Centre, Brierley Hill, and if Tramtrain technology is approved, to Stourbridge. The potential opening date being some time after 2014. The plan is for the tram tracks to diverge from the heavy rail route at Dudley and avoid the tunnel (located just to the south of the Dudley station site) so that the trams actually serve the town centre. Meanwhile the location of the station and subsequent Freightliner depot progressively becomes more overgrown, with just a hint of the closed freight line tracks on the right-hand side.
*Paul Dorney/JW (2)*

DUDLEY: Looking from Tipton Road overbridge on 14 June 1964, the last train to Birmingham Snow Hill awaits departure at 8.10pm, consisting of a scratch DMU set with Gloucester RC&W Class 122 No 55018 leading. Note the dominant Odeon cinema in the background, to the left of which is the GWR booking hall leading to the footbridge that gave access to the LMS side of the station.

An infant urban forest now dominates the location, with just a glimpse of the freight-only line that survived until 1993 and whose tracks remain in situ. Still dominating the horizon is the Odeon cinema, which is of classic art deco design and dates back to 1937. It closed in 1975, but survives as a religious assembly hall. On the right is Castle Hill, where the remains of Dudley Castle are now surrounded by another of Dudley's famous attractions, the Zoological Gardens, founded in 1937. *Michael Mensing/JW*

DUDLEY PORT LOW LEVEL was the first station north of Dudley on the South Staffordshire line to Walsall it opened in 1850 two years before the High Level station on the Stour Valley route, the two stations were connected by a footpath. In later years most Dudley trains terminated at High Level, linked to Dudley by the infamous 'Dudley Dasher' shuttle service, whilst Low Level trains served stations to Walsall. On 2 August 1963 a two-car Park Royal Class 103 DMU draws to a halt at Low Level with a Dudley to Walsall service. The Station Master's residence and booking hall provide a significant presence on the Walsall-bound platform while more basic accommodation is provided on the Dudley-bound platform. The LNWR-type signal box on the Stour Valley line dominates the background and the fencing seen above the footbridge denotes the northern end of the High Level platform.

The disused tracks are now barely visible beneath the carpet of vegetation that now envelopes the site of Low level station. Note the bridge abutments in the foreground, which show little change from the scene of 45 years ago. The footbridge is now a footpath that leads to High Level from the adjacent road. In the background, a Cross-Country Class 220 'Voyager' speeds south along the Stour Valley route, which was electrified in the 1960s. *Peter Shoesmith/JW*

GREAT BRIDGE NORTH (the 'North' was added in 1950 to differentiate it from the nearby ex-GWR station which became Great Bridge South from the same date) opened with the South Staffordshire line in 1850, and survived through to the cessation of passenger services in 1964. In essence it was more of a freight centre, with the station being squeezed into a narrow corner of the large goods yard visible to the right of a Park Royal Class 103 DMU, which is just departing with a Walsall to Dudley service on 17 May 1963. Note in the background the premises of Cashmore's, who would soon be engaged in cutting up many withdrawn BR locomotives, including several 'Duchesses', which at this time were being progressively withdrawn.

The Great Western connection from Swan Village joined the South Staffordshire's line a short distance to the south of North station, and the GWR South station was positioned just prior to that junction. The stations were just a short walk apart.

The path to the station survives today, and can clearly be identified by the iron railings (bottom left), which are probably the only remaining identifiable feature. The whole of the trackbed and platforms have been consumed by nature as has the adjacent goods yard. Although typical of the entire ex-South Staffordshire route, to see such abandonment of a location that was once so vibrant is, frankly, depressing. *Peter Shoesmith/JW*

GREAT BRIDGE, EAGLE CROSSING: The line continued north from Great Bridge towards Wednesbury, and just beyond the station was Eagle Lane level crossing, controlled in its latter days by a modern BR-design signal box, the corner of which can be seen on the right. Class 50 No 50043 *Achilles* approaches at the head of the 'Joint Line Bumper' railtour on 13 March 1982, run by F&W Railtours, the forerunner of the present-day Pathfinder Tours. The train has just passed the site of the old station, while on the left is the goods yard that by this time did not see much use. Just behind the goods office can be seen the girders of the bridge that carried the railway over a branch of the Tame Valley Canal. This was typical of many railway locations in the area, where the station was just a small part of the entire railway presence, the major role being, of course, the goods facilities.

The site of Eagle Crossing today is overwhelmed by nature, together with the constant drone of traffic from a new dual-carriageway road that now spans the area once occupied by the level crossing. The palisade fencing is proving less than effective, and the only connection that has survived the closure is the distinctive telegraph pole.
*Both JW*

47

**WEDNESBURY TOWN:** Wednesbury, together with its neighbour Darlaston, was a centre of engineering and heavy industrial excellence. A drive along the road that connects the towns would reveal names such as Patent Shaft Steelworks, Rubery Owen, Guest Keen & Nettlefold and Wilkins & Mitchell (who made Servis washing machines). Although not an area of any natural beauty, it was an area of prosperity that contributed to both the local and national economy. It was well served with railways, too, with the LMS and GWR both passing through. The LMS station dated back to the opening of the South Staffordshire route in 1850 and survived through to the cessation of passenger services in 1964. Like its Great Western rival it was known just as 'Wednesbury' until 1950, when it had 'Town' added to its title. It was marginally more convenient for the town centre, a fact of little commercial value as the two lines complemented each other rather than competed, especially for passenger business. A level crossing was situated at the southern end of the station which was also spanned by a footbridge. A Stephenson Locomotive Society special stands in the station on 2 June 1962, having just arrived with ex-LNWR 'G1' Class 0-8-0 No 48930 in charge. It is flanked by Stanier Class 8F 2-8-0 No 48726 on the centre road awaiting its next turn. In the distance a line disappears behind the Walsall-bound platform on the left, which was the freight-only 'Darlaston Loop'; this ran through the heart of the local industry to join the Grand Junction at Darlaston station. It dated back to 1863 and was essentially an avoiding line for Walsall, supporting a passenger service until 1887.

Coincidentally, this picture of Class 25 No 25038 shunting a rake of wagons in the sidings at the site of Wednesbury Town station was taken in 1977, 15 years to the day after the first. This is a Bescot 'trip' working, and has deposited the brake van on the main line while the wagons are shunted, prior to continuing towards Dudley. The Walsall-bound platform survives, but all trace of the Dudley platform has been removed. The bracket signal and level crossing gates are controlled by Wednesbury No 1 signal box, which was immediately behind the photographer. The old station's centre road has been removed, except for a short length embedded in the level crossing.

The site of the level crossing remains today, clearly pinpointing the location. Look on the extreme right and the wall that abutted the level crossing gatepost remains. Otherwise the ubiquitous Network Rail palisade fencing identifies the site of the station, although the urban forest is now well entrenched, to the extent that all background buildings are now obliterated from view.
*Peter Shoesmith/JW (2)*

WEDNESBURY TOWN: We are looking from the site of the Dudley platform at Town station. The footbridge position off the platforms indicates that its purpose was to avoid long delays to pedestrians due to the gates being closed for lengthy periods while shunting movements took place. Wednesbury No 1 signal box (by now the only signal box at Wednesbury) is on the right as Bescot's breakdown train heads back to base hauled by an unidentified Class 25 locomotive. The bridge carrying the now closed Great Western route dominates the background, with the final insult being that the once busy main line is now downgraded to a siding for stored wagons. Through the bridge is a glimpse of Ocker Hill Power Station.

Although the line has been theoretically 'mothballed', it has become very overgrown. Palisade fencing now guards the location with the embedded rail in the level crossing the only reminder of the railway to the casual visitor. The bridge that carried the GWR main line was subsequently removed, and some years later a new one erected in the same place, which now carries the Midland Metro, one piece of optimism in a now depressed area. Note the metal bracket that once supported a light, glimpsed through the trees, which is the same one that can be seen to the immediate right of the Class 25 in the earlier scene. *Both JW*

WEDNESBURY EXCHANGE SIDINGS: Beyond the GWR main line bridge, the location opens up and was dominated by the bulk of Ocker Hill Power Station which was decommissioned and demolished in 1985. It was served by the LNWR Princes End branch, which ran from Wednesbury to Bloomfield Junction, just north of Tipton on the Stour Valley line; the course of the line can be seen on the extreme left running along an embankment. In the foreground is the junction with the South Staffordshire line, which also continued south-west to Great Bridge and Dudley. Curving away sharply to the right are Wednesbury's Exchange Sidings, which lead to Wednesbury Steel Terminal. On 11 May 1977 'Peak' Class 45 No 45073 awaits departure from the exchange sidings with a rake of empty bogie tanks for Ripple Lane.

The collapse of both heavy and manufacturing industry has blighted the Black Country in general, and the Wednesbury area in particular. Most of the well-known names that dominated the area in the middle of the last century have gone, with the exception of Guest Keen & Nettlefold. As a consequence of the closure of the steel terminal the exchange sidings were lifted but instead of the scenes of desolation so prevalent elsewhere, this location today is one of regeneration. While this view is taken from only approximately where the footbridge once stood, it nevertheless looks directly into the Wednesbury Depot of the Midland Metro, its central maintenance facility. *Both JW*

WEDNESBURY EXCHANGE SIDINGS: A desolate scene, maybe, but this was the Exchange Sidings in full operation. On the left is the connection to the Great Western main line, while dropping away to the right is the connection to Wednesbury Town. Note the footbridge on the right, which is the same as that seen in the previous picture. A scrapyard occupies the land between the tracks, while the church at Hill Top can be seen on the horizon. This was a busy location, as it not only dealt with inter-regional traffic but was also the main rail artery for the Patent Shaft Steelworks, one of the major industrial concerns in Wednesbury.

The Midland Metro tram depot now occupies the site and this is the view looking in the same direction today. The Metro lines are just to the left, and follows the course of the old Great Western main line, while a car park roughly equates with the scrapyard in the earlier scene. The road out of the depot follows the course of the rail connection that once ran down to Wednesbury No 1 signal box. Trams representing the two liveries currently carried by the fleet act as a frame, with that on the right carrying the name of local footballing legend Jeff Astle, one of West Bromwich Albion's finest centre forwards. *Rob Selvey/JW*

PRINCES END (LNWR): From Wednesbury, an LNWR branch diverged from the Dudley line to wind its way via Ocker Hill and Princes End to join the Stour Valley route at Bloomfield Junction, just north of Tipton Owen Street. A little-known line, but important in its own way, its main purpose was to serve the local industry. In later years, particularly during the electrification of both the Stour Valley and Grand Junction routes, it proved to be a useful diversionary route for West Coast expresses. The branch was opened in 1863, and carried the Walsall to Wolverhampton passenger service until Pleck and Portobello Junctions enabled the trains to be transferred to the Grand Junction route. Princes End and Ocker Hill were the two stations on the route, both of which closed in 1916 with the withdrawal of passenger services. On 13 January 1979 a railtour hauled by Class 25s Nos 25040 and 25069 hurries through the site of Princes End station en route from London Marylebone to the North West.

No trace of the station remains today, and the surrounding area has also seen considerable change making it impossible to identify any connection between the two photographs. The course of the railway is now a linear walkway, so its passage through Princes End can be easily followed. This view is taken just inside what would have been Upper Church Road level crossing. *Andrew Bannister/GD*

52

PRINCES END (LNWR): Class 25 No 25138 eases across Upper Church Road level crossing at Princes End with a single brake van in tow heading for Bilston Steelworks. The signal box protects the busy level crossing beyond which is the site of Princes End (LNWR) station. The fortunes of the branch were very much tied up with the industry of the area, especially traffic generated by Bilston Steelworks. It was the closure of the latter in 1979 that spelled the end of the branch, which closed in 1981.

   The location today is a continuation of the linear walkway that passes through the old station site, and just the boundaries of the location give a hint of its previous use. No other trace of the railway remains.
*Andrew Bannister/GD*

RUSHALL LEVEL CROSSING was on the South Staffordshire line north towards Alrewas and Rugeley Town, and its position on Station Road is the best indicator of the location of this long-closed station which dated back to the opening of the line, but was closed as early as 1909. The level crossing will be remembered in more recent times for the road congestion created every time the gates were closed for a passing train. The crossing was converted to barriers a few years before closure, but it was still a gated crossing in June 1975 when Class 47 No 47234 approaches with a Tinsley to Eastleigh freight.

The section of line between Ryecroft Junction and Anglesey Sidings near Brownhills closed on 19 March 1984, and the tracks were lifted soon afterwards. The signal box didn't last too long after closure falling victim to vandalism. However, the route has been safeguarded, and in more recent years the value of the South Staffordshire line as a potential strategic freight route avoiding Birmingham has been recognised, as well as a useful commuter route linking Walsall and Lichfield. An urban walkway now utilises the course of the old line and any reinstatement of a railway remains some years off. Today part of the trackbed has been hard surfaced while the remainder has become overgrown, which is typical of the closed part of the route. A pedestrian crossing marks the site of the level crossing and the site of Rushall station has long since returned to nature. *Both JW*

PELSALL is a quiet suburb that nestles between Ryecroft Junction and Brownhills, and following the
early closure of Rushall in 1909 became the first station north of Walsall on the South Staffordshire line
to Wichnor Junction. It opened with the line in 1849 and survived until the withdrawal of the passenger
service in 1965. On a cold Christmas Eve in 1962 a northbound freight has just passed through the station
with the locomotive's exhaust being whipped away on a brisk east wind. The booking hall is a substantial
structure behind which is a small goods yard which, judging by the activity, may have been the destination
of at least some of the wagons from the freight train. An attractive latticework footbridge connects the
platforms, with a good-sized waiting shelter on the southbound platform.

There is not much around at Pelsall nowadays to indicate that it was once the location of a double track
railway and, for essentially a rural halt, a decent-sized station. Mature trees now form a guard of honour
for users of the pathway that follows the trackbed, except for a short distance on the left, which runs quite
close to Station Road. *Roger Shenton/JW*

PELSALL: The view from Pelsall station footbridge looking north provides a good vantage point to enjoy the wealth of detail in this mid-1960s scene as Stanier 'Mogul' Class 6P5F No 42957, displaying a Woodford Halse 2F shed code, clanks by on a southbound rake of mineral wagons. Positioned on the left are the two goods sidings, so typical of the time, which no doubt kept the local coal merchants in good supply. Looking beyond the railway reveals much development, with the newer houses that dominate the background contrasting with the older properties just visible on the left. It looks like a Monday judging by the well-populated washing lines, the owners of which are probably not too keen on the regular passage of steam locomotives, especially on days such as this when an easterly wind pushed the locomotive exhausts in their direction. Note the flat-roofed building immediately behind the locomotive.

Getting into the same position in 2009 was slightly problematical for two reasons: first, a clump of trees now occupies roughly the area covered by the signal and buffer stop, and, perhaps more significantly, the footbridge on which Peter Shoesmith was standing has long been demolished. Therefore this view is slightly more to the north, probably from a point close to where the telegraph pole stands, but note the square windowless building, which is the same as that situated behind the 'Mogul' in the 'past' shot. The roofs of the same house are also visible, while the land beyond the goods yard has since been utilised for further housing. *Peter Shoesmith/JW*

BROWNHILLS is probably best known to motorists as a town on the old Roman road that is now the A5 through Staffordshire, although it is now technically part of the Metropolitan Borough of Walsall. Its prosperity has ebbed and flowed on the back of coal-mining, for which it became a centre in the late 19th century with initially canal and later rail links. It was ultimately graced with two stations, the first on the Walsall to Lichfield route, which opened in 1849 and remained open until withdrawal of the passenger service in 1965. The station was positioned in a shallow cutting on the Lichfield side of the Chester Road bridge and consisted of a large booking hall and what looks very much like a Station Master's house on the Walsall-bound platform, with a wooden waiting shelter on the opposite side. Note how the southbound platform is recessed to accommodate a spur into sidings as a Class 104 two car DMU prepares to continue its journey with a Burton-upon-Trent to Wolverhampton train on 2 December 1963. Brownhills second station was on the Midland Railway's branch from Aldridge.

The urban forest has taken over the cutting where the station once stood, and no evidence of its previous existence remains from street level. The old station was well positioned for the town being situated at the west end of the High Street, and would be ideally placed if any future reopening took place. *Peter Shoesmith/JW*

BROWNHILLS: Looking south from the Chester Road bridge reveals a small goods yard on the right and sidings on the left behind the signal box, which were used for stabling coaching stock, with one rake in situ. The main-line connection to these sidings is clearly evident on the previous photograph of Brownhills station. On the main line a grubby 'Jubilee', No 45626 *Seychelles*, looks to be restarting a pick-up freight, judging the towering exhaust on a chilly-looking 2 December 1963. What looks very much like a Rover P4, now considered to be a classic car, stands in the driveway of the goods yard, beyond which stands typically solid early-20th-century terraced and detached housing.

The original bridge from which the 'past' scene was taken is now part of a traffic island, which is clearly identified by a large statue of a miner (out of picture), which stands at the 'town' end of the junction and commemorates Brownhills's connection with local coal-mining. The new bridge, created with the new traffic island, provides a slightly different perspective, which matters little as the area is as overgrown as the adjacent station site. The terraced properties on the right do help to place the location though. *Peter Shoesmith/JW*

HAMMERWICH is a small hamlet roughly midway between Brownhills and Lichfield, so the fact that it retained its station from the date the line opened in 1845 through to the cessation of passenger services in 1965 is, perhaps, a little surprising considering the demise of other stations in the area that actually served a larger community. The most significant feature was a large station house which appears to also incorporate a booking hall. Wooden waiting shelters provide basic accommodation on each platform, which are joined by a fabricated steel footbridge. On 2 December 1963 a two-car Class 101 DMU departs with a Burton-upon-Trent to Wolverhampton service. Note the portable steps to assist passengers due to the low platform height.

The station house, now extensively renovated and extended, and the footbridge survive, together with part of the single line. Note how the track has been lifted beyond the footbridge, which seems a little strange – maybe 'removed' would be a more appropriate term. The old down line was lifted some years ago, although the indentations where the sleepers lay are still very pronounced in the trackbed. *Peter Shoesmith/JW*

ANGLESEY SIDINGS, between Brownhills and Hammerwich, took their name from the Marquis of Anglesey, who was a local pit-owner of some influence. A branch from his Hammerwich and Uxbridge pits was opened in 1852, and connected with the South Staffordshire line at Anglesey Sidings. The branch ran north-west towards what is now Chasetown on the present-day Chasewater Railway heritage line, before it curved round the man-made lake at Chasewater, completed in 1797, to feed the nearby Wyrley & Essington Canal. In more recent times Charrington's established an oil distribution depot at a point where the old mineral branch diverged. The flow from Lindsey oil refinery produced upwards of three trains per week, depending on demand. When the through route closed in 1984, the spur from Lichfield to Anglesey Sidings remained open for the oil traffic. Just when all seemed settled along came the M6 Toll Road which, during its construction, severed for a time the branch and ultimately led to the closure of the oil depot. The site is now bereft of its storage tanks and oil discharge facility and used, ironically, as a road freight facility.

In the first picture, dated 8 May 1957, NCB 0-6-0ST No 8 shunts a rake of NCB wagons at Anglesey Sidings. The locomotive was built by Hunslet in 1953 and carries Works No 3807; it was one of several purchased by the National Coal Board in the post-war era to serve the Cannock Chase Coalfield. No 8 was based at Rawnsley Colliery at the northern tip of the branch from Anglesey it also spent time at Cannock Wood Colliery before being scrapped in 1967. The left-hand signal protects the level crossing across Chase Road, which runs from Watling Street at the nearby crossroads. The photograph was taken from land that became the oil distribution depot and the vantage point is the vicinity of the access gate to the site as seen in the next view.

The second picture dates from October 1982 with closure of the through route imminent. An unidentified pair of Class 20 locomotives head north with a mixed freight past Anglesey Sidings signal box. On the left is the entrance to Charrington's oil terminal, which had two sidings separated by the oil discharge valves. Steam wafting from the valves was always a sign that a delivery was due, as the pipes were pre-heated to ensure an uninterrupted flow of oil from the rail tankers to the storage tanks.

Following the closure of the through route from Lichfield to Walsall, the stub as far as Anglesey Sidings became known as 'the Brownhills branch', although in fact it was truncated a good mile and half from the town. The 'branch' ran as far as the Watling Street road bridge and was used exclusively by oil trains for Charrington's Oil Depot. At the oil depot the train had to be split as Charrington's had two sidings of restricted length. The last oil train ran on 17 May 2001 and Charrington's closed the depot permanently on 30 April 2002. The single line is barely visible from the vantage point of the Watling Street bridge on 29 October 2009, with tree growth now closing in on the trackbed. Beyond the avenue of trees the line runs onto an embankment, which is clear of vegetation, before passing over the M6 Toll Road on a quite substantial concrete and steel bridge. *Roger Shenton/JW (2)*

LICHFIELD, FOSSWAY CROSSING: On the outskirts of Lichfield the South Staffordshire route to Walsall crossed a minor road known as Fossway Crossing. The line was predominantly a freight route, although it did see passenger diversions from time to time. These were not that frequent, as when the main line through Tamworth had to be closed for engineering the normal diversionary route was via Sutton Coldfield, and it was only when both routes were blocked that the South Staffordshire line was used. The latter was also much longer that the preferred alternative via Sutton Coldfield. In the early 1970s an unidentified Class 45 'Peak' works an inter-regional express from the North East to the South West away from Lichfield. Note in the distance the distinctive three spires of Lichfield Cathedral to the left of the locomotive.

Probably the most amazing thing that the present-day view reveals is that the signal box has survived, albeit boarded up and without any steps. It may be that its somewhat remote location and a couple of residential properties close by have saved it from the fate suffered by other closed signal boxes in the area as a result of vandalism. The line was singled well before closure, but the crossing gate equipment remains in situ and looks to be in a reasonable state of repair. The cathedral spires once again pinpoint the location.
*G. F. Bannister/JW*

LICHFIELD CITY became the city's second station in 1849 with the opening of the South Staffordshire line from Walsall. From the date of opening through to the present day it enjoys one great advantage over the Trent Valley station, which had opened two years earlier to serve the Rugby to Stafford main line, in that its location is close to the city centre. Lichfield's prominence was enhanced in 1884 when the LNWR extended its Sutton Coldfield branch northwards which provided the city with a direct service to Birmingham New Street. Not surprisingly the Birmingham connection became the most important, especially in more recent times. The new line from Sutton Coldfield joined the South Staffordshire about half a mile south of the station, and the junction was controlled by Lichfield City No 1 signal box, which was positioned between the two pairs of running lines at the south end of the station. The left-hand signals on each of the brackets cover the Birmingham line, and those on the right the old South Staffordshire route, which by this time had been truncated to Anglesey Sidings. Framed between them is an approaching Class 116 DMU working a Cross City line service in the late 1980s.

The importance of Lichfield City was cemented in 1978 when it became the northern terminus of Birmingham's first Cross City line, which runs through to Redditch. It was a welcome boost, as earlier there had been rumours of the line going no further than Blake Street on the county boundary, Those suspicions were fuelled when a new turn-back facility was installed there. The line was an immediate success,

which led to expansion of services and eventually the electrification of the line in 1992. Electrification bought with it track and signalling improvements, which inevitably meant the end for Lichfield's manual signalling. Lichfield City No 1 closed on 12 October 1992, with responsibility for the entire route to Proof House Junction on the outskirts of New Street station passing to a new integrated signalling centre at Duddeston. On 9 December 2009 Class 323 No 323212 is seen departing from Lichfield City with the 10.47 Lichfield Trent Valley to Redditch service. *Both JW*

LICHFIELD CITY: In a tranquil scene looking back into the north end of Lichfield City station on 20 August 1967, several sets of DMUs are stabled awaiting their next turn of duty. At this time DMUs were stabled overnight at Lichfield in order to form early peak-hour services the following morning thus avoiding the need for empty stock workings from Tyseley, where the units were based. This being a Sunday means that probably more DMUs are stabled than normal, it also explains the wagons standing in Platform 1, indicating that engineers have a possession in progress. There were two sizable goods yards on each side of the station, together with a large goods shed on the down side. Note the crane positioned in the yard next to the wagons. In the foreground is Lichfield City No 2 signal box, positioned at the end of the lengthy island platforms, while beyond the station canopy and signal gantry No 1 signal box is just visible. Examples of Metro-Cammell Class 101 and Derby Class 116 DMUs are the main types stabled awaiting the following morning's rush-hour.

The new order at Lichfield City is represented by Class 323 EMU No 323212 heading north for Trent Valley on the final leg of its journey with the 0933 service from Longbridge. The layout was simplified when the line was electrified, although the goods yard on the left had already closed by that time. The sidings on the right have also been lifted as overnight stabling of units was discontinued more than 20 years ago, while the goods shed is now a tyre distribution centre. The station remains virtually unaltered, and in recent times has received a welcome makeover that has greatly improved both its appearance and its facilities. Note that the old goods yard is being redeveloped with apartment blocks. *Roger Shenton/JW*

SHENSTONE: The only intermediate station on the Cross City line between Lichfield and the West Midlands boundary is at Shenstone. Its station, which dates back to 1884, retains a lot of character as the imposing booking hall on the up (Birmingham) platform has been kept together with its canopy, the latter surviving the electrification of the line. It is only on the down platform that the old waiting room has been removed and now only basic 'bus-stop'-style shelters are provided. One casualty of electrification was the footbridge, which was replaced by new pedestrian access to each platform from the road bridge. Looking towards the station from the Footherley Road bridge on a chilly January morning in the early 1980s reveals the remnants of Shenstone's goods yard with the large goods shed still extant. It had closed some years earlier, and had been given over to non-railway-related business use. The substantial station building can be seen in the background as a diverted express from Derby to Bristol, hauled by a Class 47 locomotive, accelerates ahead of the climb to Blake Street.

A small housing development now occupies the site of the goods yard, but it is pleasing to note that the station remains unchanged, and in recent years the unoccupied part of the building has been let, which has had the effect of protecting its fabric. The station is served by a half-hourly service between Lichfield and Birmingham New Street, and on 23 November 2009 Class 323 EMU No 323207 heads for New Street and Redditch with the 13.47 service from Lichfield Trent Valley. *Both JW*

ALREWAS station was situated just to the south of Wichnor Junction on the South Staffordshire line to Lichfield and Walsall, and dated back to 1849. This scene shows the station just prior to closure in 1965 as a northbound diverted express hauled by a Class 45 'Peak' locomotive passes through en route for Derby. The level crossing at the northern end of the station was controlled by Alrewas signal box, situated behind the photographer.

The station was situated on the eastern edge of Alrewas with the A38 trunk road running virtually alongside the railway, while the village was just a short distance away across the A38. However, when this road was turned into a dual carriageway, the site of the station became very remote from the village with virtually no satisfactory pedestrian access. However, another significant local development may yet aid the reopening of the line, and Alrewas station, to passenger trains. Nearby has been created the National Arboretum, a dedicated memorial to the armed forces which is becoming an ever more popular attraction, to the extent that a campaign has been started to provide rail access. Currently little traffic uses the stretch of line between Wichnor Junction and Lichfield Trent Valley High Level Junction, where the Cross City line now commences, together with the chord down to the Trent Valley line. *Phil Waterfield/GD*

BLOXWICH: The South Staffordshire Railway's second route from Ryecroft Junction through to Cannock opened on 1 February 1858, and after the closure of a station at Birchills in 1916 Bloxwich became the first station on the route. The town, which has a mention in the Domesday Book, grew in the 18th century from a village to an industrial town due both to mining and manufacture. The original station was located a short walk from the town centre and consisted of a booking hall with a canopy on the up side and a waiting shelter on the down side, a goods yard with a sizable shed was provided. On a rather misty 27 March 1964 a Metro-Cammell Class 101 two-car DMU calls with a service for Rugeley, while an unidentified ex-LNWR Class 7F 0-8-0 trundles through on the up line, no doubt heading for Bescot. The station closed on 18 January 1965 with the withdrawal of passenger services on that date as part of the Beeching 'axe', although the last passenger train to use the station was an excursion on 29 May 1966. Demolition followed soon afterwards.

Today the track formation remains very similar to the 1964 scene, and the location of the station is clearly evident on the right-hand side. The goods shed survives in good condition, still with the three strengthening bars evident on the side elevation. Bloxwich signal box controls the very busy level crossing, situated just behind the photographer, as well as a mixture of colour light and semaphore signals. On the Walsall side of the crossing a short spur runs into industrial premises, now alas unused and scheduled for closure. When the passenger service was reinstated in 1989 a new station was provided some 500 metres north of the old one, located closer to two sizable housing estates but not, unlike the old station, so convenient for the town centre. The new station, which is just visible beyond the background bridge, is of only basic construction and compares very unfavourably with the neat and pleasing appearance of the original. On 28 October 2009 a Class 170/153 combination with No 170516 leading passes the site of the old station with the 1206 service from Rugeley Trent Valley to Birmingham New Street. *Peter Shoesmith/JW*

CANNOCK was the northern terminal of the South Staffordshire Railway for a short period, and the station was opened at the same time as the line in 1858. In later years it reflected the LNWR influence in its buildings, which present an attractive vista as a local service from Walsall to Rugeley draws in on 13 May 1963, consisting of a pair of two-car Park Royal Class 103 DMUs. The attractive booking hall is situated on the town side of the station, while a wooden waiting shelter is provided on the opposite platform. A spur to the goods yard is evident adjacent to the signal box, and the station has the added luxury of a through centre road. It closed with the withdrawal of passenger services in January 1965, although the route remained open for freight traffic that, in subsequent years, was to become quite sparse, and as a diversionary route when either the Grand Junction or the Trent Valley lines were closed for engineering.

The new station is functional, unstaffed with two basic platforms and just 'bus-stop'-style waiting shelters providing the minimum accommodation for travellers. It is a pity, because Cannock is a good-sized town and deserves better. Another significant difference is that it no longer has a through centre road. Looking at the formation as dictated by a bridge parapet just behind the approaching train, the new up platform stands where once the up platform road was situated. On 29 October 2009 Class 170 No 170517 eases up the gradient on the approach to the station with the 1407 service from Birmingham New Street to Hednesford. *Peter Shoesmith/JW*

HEDNESFORD: The gap between the South Staffordshire's Walsall to Cannock line, which opened in 1858, and the Trent Valley route, which had opened 11 years earlier, was closed in 1859 by the Cannock Mineral Railway. This line's initial more grandiose plans for a railway from Uttoxeter through to Wolverhampton had been scaled back, but nevertheless the 'infill' provided the LNWR, to whom it was leased, with yet another valuable route. Hednesford was the first new station north of Cannock, and also became a railhead catering for several local collieries. There were numerous rafts of sidings surrounding the station to deal with the coal traffic on which the town based its prosperity. This is Hednesford in Edwardian times, with an LNWR Webb 2-4-2T standing at the head of a train for Walsall. Note the impressive station booking hall perched on the road bridge. The platforms extended on both sides of the bridge; a short canopy can be seen just beyond the abutment. It is a bustling scene that looks like the morning commute for many of the passengers to Walsall, or even Birmingham.

The original station closed in 1965 and the line was used for freight and passenger diversions until 1989 when, after much pressure, Hednesford became the northern terminus of a new passenger service, initially from Walsall then soon afterwards, due to its success, Birmingham New Street. The up platform had survived and was brought back into use; the down platform had been removed and a replacement was necessary when the service was extended to Rugeley Town in 1997. As with other stations on the route, it is unmanned and offers the most basic of shelters on each platform. The road bridge has been rebuilt, the sidings on the left lifted and the land now used for a housing development. Hednesford retains semaphore signalling, and the signal box is located just beyond the bridge; it is one of three on the line, the other two being Bloxwich and Brereton Sidings at Rugeley Town both of which are due to be replaced in 2010 when the new Saltley Signalling Panel is brought into use. Heading for Rugeley Trent Valley is a Class 170/153 combination, with No 170507 at the rear, forming the 1139 service from Birmingham New Street on 4 December 2009. *Mrs T. B. Dudley, collection of John Bucknall/JW*

HEDNESFORD: West Cannock Colliery dominated the landscape to the north of Hednesford and was a major source of traffic up until its closure in 1977. Its access to the Cannock Chase line was guarded by Hednesford No 3 signal box, of LNWR design and dating back to 1923, the year of the Grouping when the LNWR became part of the LMS. The curiosity was that it retained lower-quadrant LNWR-pattern signal until the early 1970s, as evident in this 1971 scene, which also provides a good view of the signal box itself as well as Class 47 No 1721 hauling a diverted West Coast express to London Euston. The tall signal post was to give drivers adequate warning; the Home signal was controlled by No 3 box, and the Distant No 2 box.

The closure of the colliery also spelled the end of Hednesford No 3 signal box, which spent its last days switched out. The old LNWR post was replaced by a plain Distant signal. Eventually the signal box was closed permanently and now just the sweeping curve remains of what was once a busy junction. The site of the colliery is now parkland. On 19 November 2009 Class 153 No 153354 leads Class 170 No 170513 forming the 1306 service from Rugeley Trent Valley to Birmingham New Street. *G. F. Bannister/JW*

RUGELEY TOWN station opened on 1 June 1870 when the extension of the line from Cannock was completed by the Cannock Mineral Railway, which soon after leased the line to the LNWR. It was centrally located for the town, perched at the top of an embankment next to the bridge that carries the railway over the busy A51 Lichfield to Stoke-on-Trent road. A two-car Class 101 DMU approaches with a Stafford to Birmingham New Street working. Note in the background the spur into Rugeley Power Station. The main line swings to the left behind the DMU, it will then shortly connect with the Trent Valley line.

The new Rugeley Town station, which opened in 1997 when the 'Chase Line' was extended from Hednesford, is situated a short distance to the south of the original. In fact, the train, consisting of a Class 170/153 combination with No 170508 leading, has just passed the site of the old station. As with all the other stations on the line from Walsall, it is unmanned and consists of just the most basic of accommodation, although it does have its own car park. Train services now run through to Rugeley Trent Valley, which is about a mile to the north. *Peter Shoesmith/JW*

ALDRIDGE: We are now back on the Midland route from Wolverhampton through Sutton Park, which joined the Birmingham to Derby main line at Park Lane Junction, between Water Orton and Castle Bromwich. Aldridge was the first station east of Walsall and dated back to 1879; it was one of five on the route, the others being Streetley, Sutton Park, Sutton Town and Penns. Until 1930 passenger trains also ran from Aldridge onto the branch to Brownhills, the junction for which was at the Walsall end of the station. Aldridge enjoyed a passenger service until 1965 when it was withdrawn as part of the 'Beeching Plan', which decimated local train services in the area. The station is unusually busy on 12 December 1964 as the SLS 'Farewell to LNWR Locomotives' railtour, featuring ex-LNWR 0-8-0s Class 'G2' No 49430 and Class 'G2A' No 49361, pauses for a photographic stop. The goods yard can be seen behind the station, while the goods shed (far left) identifies the course of the Brownhills branch.

All trace of the station has long since been swept away, and the goods yard is now a housing development. It is ironic that at the time the passenger service was withdrawn the local housing stock was increasing due to Aldridge's convenient location for both Walsall, Sutton Coldfield and Birmingham. Reinstatement of passenger services over the 'Sutton Park line' has been mooted, and the site of the station has not been totally redeveloped. The line remains busy with freight traffic, as evident on 25 November 2009 as EWS Class 66 No 66213 passes the station site with an engineer's train from Bescot to Toton. *Paul Dorney/JW*

WALSALL WOOD: The branch from Aldridge to Brownhills was opened by the Midland Railway in 1882, initially as a freight line aimed at tapping the lucrative business created by the local coal mines. A passenger service along the branch followed two years later with stations at Walsall Wood and the inconveniently sited Brownhills (Midland). The passenger service did not thrive and was withdrawn in 1930, although freight services continued until the early 1960s. In September 1957 a Fowler 0-6-0 is seen shunting mineral wagons to the north of the station.

The course of the railway has been secured for recreational use and a children's play area is now the feature. The station building survived the closure and lifting of the branch by a few years, at least until the late 1960s, as it had passed into commercial use. The branch closed in two stages, initially north of Walsall Wood to Brownhills in 1960. Its main problem was that it was a poor relation of the nearby LNWR route, which served roughly the same area and whose Brownhills station was much more centrally located for the town. *Peter Shoesmith/JW*

WALSALL WOOD COLLIERY: A colliery was founded at Walsall Wood in 1874 when the first shafts were sunk, and mining was to continue on the site until 1964, when the supply of accessible coal was exhausted. Although not the first colliery in the area – a pit at nearby Shelfield had existed since 1851 – the newcomer made an impact on the hitherto small community, both in terms of increased population due to the influx of miners and their families and also in the provision of public services to meet their demands. The colliery was situated about a mile north of the station, and as can be seen, the pithead winding gear and other buildings were tucked away behind a spoil heap. This view from Coppice Road looks down on the site and shows the Midland Railway's line to Brownhills diverging to the left, with a spur branching off into the colliery. Kitson 0-6-0ST No 5036 of 1913, which carries the name *Griffin*, is seen running light towards the exchange sidings on the far side of the bridge, close to the station. The locomotive had previously served at Cannock Wood Colliery and was withdrawn and scrapped in 1963.

Like many bridges that once spanned now closed railways, the Coppice Lane bridge that overlooked Walsall Wood Colliery has been taken out, with only a slight rise in the roadway to give any hint of its existence. Equally, the land looking towards the colliery site also betrays no evidence that a mine and railway once occupied this location. A combination of residential apartment blocks and an industrial unit are now in situ. *Peter Shoesmith/JW*

# Wolverhampton and the
# Great Western main line

WOLVERHAMPTON LOW LEVEL: The Great Western Railway reached Wolverhampton in 1854 by way of the Oxford, Worcester & Wolverhampton line. This was followed later the same year by the Birmingham Wolverhampton & Dudley Railway, which brought the important connection to Birmingham Snow Hill and onwards to Paddington, thus providing Wolverhampton with its second direct route via Birmingham to London. The LNWR's line via New Street to Euston had opened two years earlier. By way of the Wolverhampton Junction Railway, which also opened in 1854, the GWR also gained access to the Shrewsbury & Birmingham Railway. Of significance, Wolverhampton also became the northern limit of the broad gauge, as the lines opened before the Act then before Parliament halting its future expansion became law. The station opened on 1 July 1854, adopting the title 'Low Level' two years later to differentiate it from its elevated LNWR next-door neighbour. Originally it had an overall roof, of Brunel design, which was removed in 1922. We are looking into Low level from the north end of the down main platform in around 1905, which gives a good impression of the length of the station. Like Snow Hill in Birmingham it had been built with long and wide platforms so that each could accommodate two trains simultaneously, thus greatly improving the flexibility of the station. The line is curving out to pass beneath the Wednesfield Road bridge, while positioned in the centre roads are a rake of clerestory coaches with distinctive running boards, adjacent is a rake of vans. The footbridge stands proud in the background and a sole clerestory coach is positioned in the bay platform on the extreme right. On the extreme left can be glimpsed the roof of the carriage shed, between which and the station ran a through goods loop.

Today the redevelopment at the 'Shrewsbury' end of the station looks complete. On the left is 'The Bluebrick', a pub and restaurant that takes its name from the blue bricks used in millions by the builders of the railway between Low level and Snow Hill, and actually beyond to Bordesley. On the right is a Premier Inn, and looking through the space that was once occupied by the middle road is the 'Broad Gauge' apartment block, its name reflecting Wolverhampton as the northern boundary of Brunel's broad gauge. The centrepiece is an imposing work of art depicting a cylinder, from which has been cut the image of a railway guard waving his flag for 'right away'. Note the footbridge, which has been retained as part of the redevelopment. *John Alsop collection/JW*

**WOLVERHAMPTON LOW LEVEL:** This is the scene at the south (Birmingham) end of the station, also around 1905 and showing the overall roof to good effect. Stabled on the middle roads are 'Bulldog' Class 4-4-0 No 3310 *St Just* (which was a rebuild of 'Duke' Class No 3286) and Wolverhampton-built '517' Class 0-4-2T No 550. The clerestory coach on the left is stabled in the down bay platform.

The second view shows Low Level as most would like to remember it, with the centre roads occupied with a variety of passenger and parcels stock as ex-Great Western 'Castle' 4-6-0 No 5070 *Sir Daniel Gooch* awaits departure with the up 'Cambrian Coast Express' to London Paddington on 12 October 1961.

In the third photograph the end is nigh: two years before the cessation of passenger services on 6 March 1972 the station also had become a Parcels Depot, and it remained thus until 1981. This was followed by five years in the hands of the Divisional Engineer's Department until May 1986 when the site became the property of Wolverhampton Council. Many plans were floated for the site, one being the terminus of the Midland Metro, which was to follow the trackbed of the old main line through to Birmingham Snow Hill, another was a transport museum. In addition to parcels stock, the station was home for a short while to preserved Class 25 No 25067, seen here at the head of two parcels vans and a Mark 1 coach on 16 June 1984. By this time the tracks had been truncated just short of the footbridge and a new platform created where the centre roads had once stood. The fabric of the station looks to be in remarkably good condition and

the location of the two bay platforms is clearly evident. Some track of the through goods line, which was located between the station and the carriage shed, is still in situ and looks to be in use for stabling parcels stock. By this time the only main-line connection was to the Walsall line. The Class 25 was removed soon after to Swindon, and happily is now in active preservation on the Battlefield Line, based at Shackerstone. Wolverhampton High Level station can be seen in the background.

Although the railway has long since gone, and with the scars of redevelopment everywhere, Low Level seems to be retaining the essence of a railway station. This is the view from what was once Sun Street overbridge, which spanned the station throat and has been levelled as part of the redevelopment. The down platform and its canopy has been retained, and behind it is the Grade 1-listed station booking hall and offices. The latter is a larger version of the station buildings that were typical of the route to Birmingham Snow Hill, and to this date it retains an imposing presence, albeit in the middle of a building site. Looking to the right, the up platform can still be identified and, more importantly, so can the impressive blue-brick retaining wall, which once supported the overall roof. *John Alsop collection/John Dew/JW (2)*

WOLVERHAMPTON LOW LEVEL: The end of steam is nigh in this mid-1960s view, framed by the Wednesfield Road bridge, as a grimy BR Standard Class 5 4-6-0, unidentified due to having lost its smokebox number plate, draws away with a down service, probably for Shrewsbury and beyond. On the left a Brush Type 4 diesel (later Class 47) is arriving with an up working, while the down bays are occupied by a BR Class 08 shunter and an English Electric Type 4 diesel (later Class 40), which appears to be attached to a parcels van. The reporting code of 1M02 indicates an inter-regional Class 1 working. Class 40s were common at Low Level in the early-to-mid-1960s hauling diverted London Midland Region expresses during engineering possessions in connection with the electrification of the Stour Valley and Grand Junction routes. Note the flat roof of Wolverhampton power signal box and the gabled roof of Mill Street Goods Depot, both visible above the cab roof of the Class 08 shunter.

It is not possible to use the Wednesfield Road bridge as a frame nowadays, for the simple reason that it has been filled in, and the road level looks to have been eased as well. The Premier Inn now occupies part of the down side of the old station, with The Bluebrick pub to its left. However, on the extreme right is the unmistakable retaining wall that supports the embankment on which High Level station is positioned. In the distance is the flat roof of the power signal box, and behind it remains the gabled roof of Mill Street Goods Depot. *Brian Robbins/JW*

WOLVERHAMPTON LOW LEVEL: A glance at the huge retaining wall supporting the embankment that accommodates High Level station will reveal a series of arches, which identify the location of 'the arcade', which is a walkway built into the retaining wall to provide access from Low Level station via a pedestrian tunnel beneath the LNWR lines to High Level station and the city centre (city status was granted in 2000). Equally, the walkway provided a grandstand view of the northern end of Low level station, where begrimed 'Castle' 4-6-0 No 7024 *Powis Castle* stands in the middle road in readiness to take over a working to Shrewsbury. In the background, beyond the parapet of Wednesfield Road bridge, the unmistakable shape of Butlers Springfield Brewery can be seen. Note the trolleybus poles supporting the overhead wiring.

Wolverhampton, like its neighbour Walsall, operated a fleet of trolleybuses and the route to Wednesfield was one of its busiest.

A car park now occupies the throat of what was once Low Level station, serving the hotel and pub that have been built at the north end of the station site. Of specific note is that the Wednesfield Road bridge has been filled in and only the embankment retaining wall on the far side betrays any evidence of the site's previous role. The trolleybus poles have also long since gone, and on the left is an apartment block built on the trackbed on the far side of Wednesfield Road. The charred remains of Butlers Springfield Brewery are just visible beyond what was once the railway bridge. *John Bucknall/JW*

79

A glance over the wall of Lock Street today reveals a completely different vista. The entire trackbed between Wednesfield Road bridge and a footbridge that crossed the Low Level tracks at the end of Lock Street is occupied by a multi-storey office and apartment complex, which even provides a basketball court for its residents, roughly situated in the same place once occupied by the Standard Class 5! The Premier Inn building dominates the background, next to which is the retaining wall of the High Level alignment. *Brian Robbins/JW*

WOLVERHAMPTON LOW LEVEL: A begrimed BR Standard Class 5 clanks beneath Wednesfield Road bridge at the head of a Shrewsbury working, watched by a group of railwaymen on the left, beneath the banner repeater signal. To the far left a Stanier 'Black 5' is seen running into the up platform. This image reflects the twilight of steam at Low Level and dates back to the mid-1960s. The 'Kings' have been gone a few years since, and just a few 'Castles' remain. Steam activity is more likely to be of LMS or Standard British Railway types, with diesel traction now predominant on the Paddington and South Coast expresses. This view is recorded from Lock Street, a cul-de-sac sandwiched between the High and Low Level tracks.

WOLVERHAMPTON LOW LEVEL: Just beyond the Wednesfield Road was a footbridge providing an effective short-cut for shoppers and football fans heading for the nearby Molineux ground, home of Wolverhampton Wanderers. This view is looking north towards Cannock Road sidings, from where ex-Great Western 'King' Class 4-6-0 No 6014 *King Henry VII* has just departed with the empty stock for a London Paddington express. This locomotive was unique within its class, as it had a wedge-shaped cab roof, the result of an early GWR streamlining exercise in 1935, the most striking feature of which was a 'half-ball'-shaped casing covering the front of the smokebox. The experiment lasted eight years. Butlers Springfield Brewery is on the right, which remains a landmark despite being gutted by fire in 2004, some 13 years after closure. The sidings on the right, known affectionately as 'The Rhubarb', were used to bring hops into the brewery, and any spillages were quickly seized upon by local railwaymen with gardens, as the hops were reputed to have a magnificent effect on their rhubarb! The brewery occupied most of the land to the right of the railway up to the distant bridge, which carries Cannock Road into the city centre.

The scene looking towards Cannock Road today is in stark contrast to that of the early 1960s, as the footbridge has now been removed and replaced by a simple staircase. The brewery is a sorry sight following the disastrous fire, although the clock tower (seen behind the signal gantry in the earlier photograph) survives; hopefully a realistic redevelopment plan will save for posterity what remains of the building. On the left is the vehicle access point (off Lock Street), from which the picture of No 6014 was taken. A scrapyard occupied the land for several years following the removal of the tracks, but now the whole alignment as far as Cannock Road and beyond is derelict. *John Bucknall/JW*

WOLVERHAMPTON LOW LEVEL: An unidentified BR Standard Class 5 4-6-0 heads away from Low Level and approaches Cannock Road bridge. The 1M12 headcode indicates that it is an inter-regional working and has probably originated on the South Coast. The type of locomotive and all-maroon stock firmly places this in the mid-1960s. The train is passing the Springfield Brewery on the left, where the legend proudly proclaims that its products are the 'Pride of the Midlands', the latter word being obscured by the locomotive's safety valve blowing off furiously. The sidings on the right are probably those of the District Engineer. Note the stepladders being used for access to the coach on the right.

Despite the fire that destroyed much of the brewery, several large buildings remain, and it is good to see that the 'Pride of the Midlands' proclamation survives, although weathering is revealing also the word 'Wolverhampton', which relates to a previous era. The shallow railway cutting has been filled in and in the background can be seen the new office and apartment blocks that occupy the trackbed on the approach to Low Level. *Brian Robbins/JW*

WOLVERHAMPTON LOW LEVEL: Until the mid-1960's looking north from Cannock Road bridge would have revealed an expanse of sidings full of coaching stock to cover both long-distance express passenger as well as suburban local services on the old Great Western lines radiating from Low Level. All this finished when the electrification of the LMR line was completed in 1967 when all through workings were transferred to the newly energised lines. Cannock Road was severely rationalised, but was still regularly used by 'merry-go-round' coal trains for Ironbridge Power Station. For several years such trains from the north continued to use Cannock Road, as the locomotive would need to run round its train in each direction. On 9 August 1973 Class 50 No D408 is seen working in from Bushbury Junction with a loaded train. It will need to reverse its train onto the siding on the left, run round, then follow the old GWR route towards Shrewsbury, which can be seen curving off to the left ahead of the gas holder. The use of a Class 50 locomotive was unusual; the class was being evaluated for potential future use on these trains following the loss of passenger work on the LMR with the onset of electrification north of Crewe. The trial came to nought, and the class was eventually transferred en masse to the Western Region; as No 50008, D408 was subsequently named *Thunderer*. The locomotive is now preserved and currently resident on the Nene Valley Railway.

The operating of 'merry-go-round' trains to and from Ironbridge from the north was greatly eased in 1983 when a new spur was built from Oxley to Bushbury Junction, which obviated the need for trains to use Cannock Road to run round. This was the final curtain for the remnant of the Low Level line, the tracks were removed and the entire area that was once Cannock Road carriage-sidings has now returned to nature. The only connecting feature between the two photographs is the canal and lock gates, which can be seen on the extreme left. Today the scene is dominated by the refuse incinerator plant, located on the inside of the curve of the former Great Western route. *G. J. Bannister/JW*

WOLVERHAMPTON LOCOMOTIVE WORKS: A locomotive works was founded at Stafford Road, Wolverhampton, by the Shrewsbury & Birmingham Railway in 1849. In 1854 it was taken over by the Great Western Railway, which made Wolverhampton responsible for its 'Northern Division'. Both locomotive construction and repair was initially undertaken, although locomotive construction ceased in 1908 when its facilities were concentrated on repairs and overhauls. The Works was expanded in 1933, with new erecting shops being constructed on the opposite side of Stafford Road. However the decision to finish with steam on the national network eventually spelled the end for the Works, which was progressively run down over the ensuing years until on a fateful 11 February 1964 '2800' Class 2-8-0 No 2859 was out-shopped as the last locomotive to be overhauled at Wolverhampton, and the Works closed. During a Works visit a few years prior to closure, a number of locomotives are seen under repair in the erecting shop which was one of the new facilities provided in the 1933 extension. '4500' Class 2-6-2T 'Prairie' No 5565 is present with its cab removed, and behind it stands a BR Standard Tank. To the right is a boiler under repair, while another 'Prairie' can be seen on the left, together with an unidentified tender locomotive.

Following closure, the site was sold off. Today an industrial estate stands on the site, which is bordered by the main line from Wolverhampton High Level to Shrewsbury. The photograph is taken at right angles to the position of the erecting shops in order to describe the scene today more effectively. *Peter Shoesmith/GD*

WOLVERHAMPTON STAFFORD ROAD SHED: Ex-Great Western engines rest at Stafford Road shed in the early 1960s. '4073' Class 'Castle' No 5046 *Earl Cawdor* and '4900' series 'Hall' No 4902 *Aldenham Hall* stand outside the main shed awaiting their next turn of duty. The locomotive depot was located within a triangular parcel of land bordered by Stafford Road itself, the main line from Shrewsbury and Dunstall Park station, and the LNWR line to Stafford. Originally it was part of the locomotive works, but with the latter's expansion it eventually had most of the site to itself. Consisting of three main roundhouses, each with its own turntable, it also had two further sheds without turntables at the rear. A traverser was also located at the back, close to the Shrewsbury main line. It was a top link shed and had an allocation of 'King' Class locomotives for its principal turns, the Paddington expresses, right up to the date of their withdrawal in 1962. The end of the 'Kings' also meant the end for Stafford Road, which closed the following year. Its remaining stud of steam locomotives were transferred to the nearby Oxley shed, on which site now stands Alstom's carriage depot.

As with much redundant ex-railway land in urban areas, the site is now given over to an industrial estate. This is the present view looking towards where the three main roundhouses stood, which would have been the on the left-hand side, while straight ahead in the background is the embankment that carries the 'Oxley Chord', which at this point follows the course of the old Great Western line. It was also the position of Dunstall Park station. *Peter Shoesmith/ GD*

85

CODSALL is situated on the north-west fringe of Wolverhampton, on the Shrewsbury line. It is unusual that both it, and nearby Bilbrook, have both survived to the present day even though the distance between them is little more than a mile. While Bilbrook is quite basic, Codsall boasts a classic Great Western station, seen here in March 1954 with Churchward 2-8-0 No 2802 bursting through on an up freight. It now enjoys a regular-interval service between Wolverhampton and Shrewsbury.

The station is not totally original as the footbridge is not the original listed structure that having been severely damaged by the jib of a contractor's crane in 2005. The remains were removed and although some parts of the bridge were salvaged for reuse, five of the original cast-iron columns were beyond repair. New columns were cast locally, and a replacement bridge in the style of the old one was restored to the station in 2008. Until 2006 the station was controlled by a manual signal box controlling semaphore signals, but now the entire route has been resignalled and is controlled by a panel at Madeley Junction, near Telford. The station is unstaffed and the main building is now used as a public house, which is reported to maintain fine ales, just waiting rooms serve the platforms. On 10 December 2009 Class 67 No 67010 passes beneath the new footbridge with the 11.27 Wrexham to London Marylebone service. *Geoff Bannister/GD*

PRIESTFIELD JUNCTION: On the outskirts of Wolverhampton the two major GWR lines from Birmingham Snow Hill and Dudley converged at Priestfield Junction before continuing to Low Level station. On 28 April 1962 'Prairie' '5100' Class 2-6-2T No 4173 arrives at Priestfield with the 1.55pm service from Stourbridge Junction. The 'main line' from Birmingham Snow Hill is seen curving in from the left. This view is taken from the footbridge, which spanned all the running lines, and shows the station to have had rudimentary accommodation for passengers.

The original station closed in two phases, with the Dudley and Stourbridge lines succumbing in 1962 when the passenger service was withdrawn from that route, while the Birmingham line soldiered on until 1972. The site then lay dormant and derelict until 1999 when the Midland Metro route opened. In the interim, the course of the Dudley line, which ran through a cutting as it passed through the station, has been completely filled in. *John Dew/GD*

# Great Western in the Black Country

BILSTON CENTRAL, the second station from Wolverhampton on the Snow Hill line, was typical of other stations on the route with the main station building on the up platform and the footbridge at the Birmingham end. It differed, however, in that the signal box was situated off the platform on the down side at the Birmingham end and was adjacent to a small goods yard situated behind the platform on the up side. In later years it appears also to have had its canopy replaced by a more modern but relatively featureless design with a flat roof. There was a small brick-built waiting shelter on the down side, which was also provided with a small canopy. Like its neighbours, Bilston's growth and importance arose from local industry, particularly Stewarts & Lloyds Steelworks which was situated about a mile from the town centre and was one of the region's largest industrial concerns; its closure in 1979 was a major blow for the community. Like all the other stations on the route, closure came in March 1972, but some years earlier, just before the end of steam in the area, an unidentified 0-6-0 pannier tank locomotive scurries through on the up line, while a Class 116 DMU has just departed for Wolverhampton Low Level with a local service from Birmingham Snow Hill.

Midland Metro tram No 16 climbs away from Bilston Central Metro stop on 30 November 2009 with a service for Birmingham Snow Hill. It is just passing the site of the old Central station, of which nothing remains except for some raised earthworks on the up side where the platform once stood. The background bridge carries the dual-carriageway Black Country Spine Road over the Metro tracks, and the tram stop is actually just visible in the shadows of the brick-lined cutting beyond the bridge. The original road bridge, which the DMU in the earlier shot is just approaching, remains but is now hidden from view by the new road. *Peter Shoesmith/Robin Banks*

**WEDNESBURY CENTRAL:** Wednesbury's second station opened in 1854, some four years after its South Staffordshire neighbour, a short walk away. The suffix 'Central' was added in 1950, although it took a little geographical licence as it was slightly further from the town centre than its rival, but it did benefit from being situated on the Great Western main line and consequently had direct links to the two major centres of Birmingham and Wolverhampton. It consisted of the traditional (for the route) block-style booking hall and station house with a signal box positioned on the Wolverhampton end of the up platform. The down side had a brick-built waiting room, behind which were situated the exchange sidings. This scene shows the station in its latter years, but before its decline with the withdrawal of through services. A Derby-built Class 116 DMU calls with a train for Birmingham Snow Hill on 12 December 1963. Of note are the pre-cast concrete lamp posts and – an icon of the age – a motor scooter, which is parked in the right-hand corner. In many respects the station design mirrors that of nearby West Bromwich.

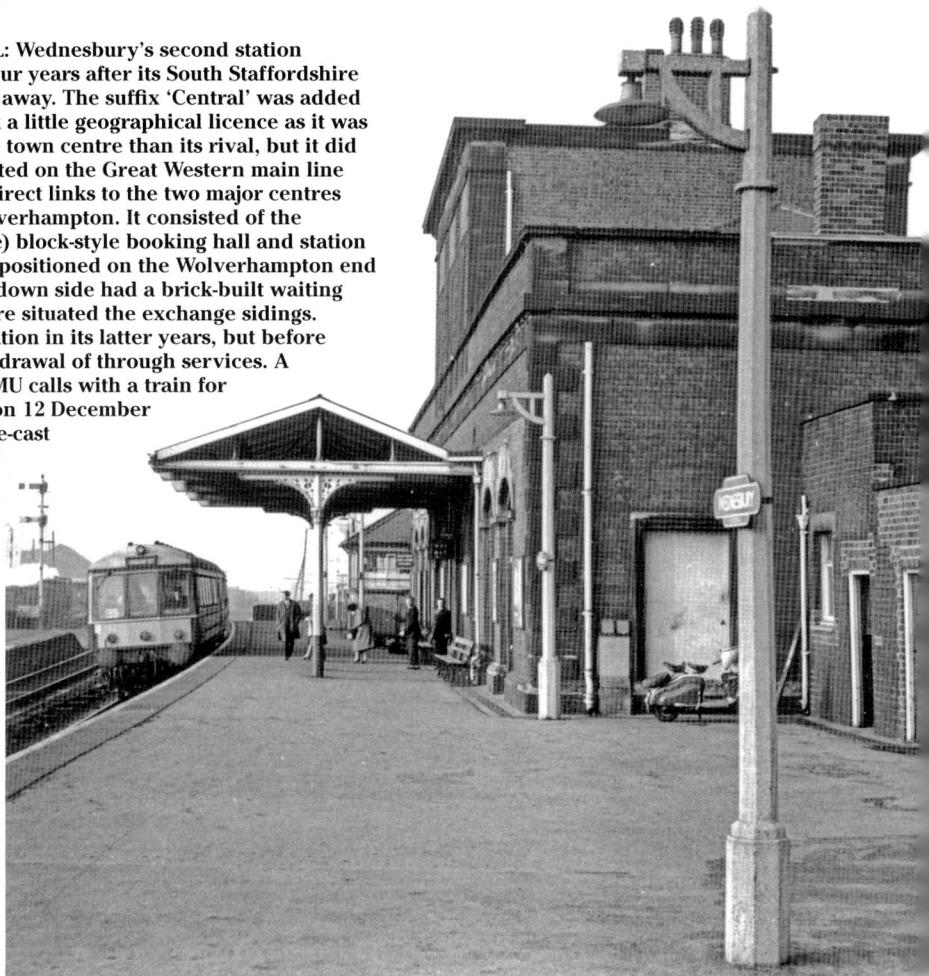

Wednesbury Great Western Street Midland Metro tram stop now occupies the site of the old station, of which nothing remains. Not only is it a tram stop, but beyond on the 'down side' lies the Midland Metro's depot which looks after the maintenance of the tram fleet. The curve of the track is consistent with the old main line as tram No 10 approaches with a service from Wolverhampton St George's to Birmingham Snow Hill on 7 November 2009.
*Peter Shoesmith/JW*

SWAN VILLAGE: The delightfully named Swan Village does not quite live up to its name, being situated in the heart of the industrial belt on the west side of West Bromwich. It was a junction station with a branch diverging from the main line to Great Bridge. On 13 June 1964 'Modified Hall' 4-6-0 No 6976 *Graythwaite Hall* heads for Wolverhampton with a down fitted freight. The station buildings differed from most others on the line as, until 1958, they consisted of attractive wooden structures with an integral canopy that formed an extension of the pitched roof. These were replaced by more mundane BR block-style buildings. The booking hall served both the main line and the Great Bridge branch, which can be seen to the right of the locomotive. The background overbridge carried Bilhay Lane and spanned the junction, as well as providing access to the platforms. A level crossing was located at the western end of both stations, each protected by its own signal box.

The Swan Village tram stop is now sited on the Wednesbury side of the level crossing, and looking in the opposite direction towards the site of the old station the key features that still identify the location are the gas-holder on the right and the background Bilhay Road overbridge. The station site has been levelled and a walkway now follows the Metro tram tracks on the old up side. The surrounding area remains a mix of domestic housing and industry. Tram No 10 is seen passing through the site of the old Swan Village station with a Wolverhampton-bound service on 30 November 2009. *Paul Dorney/JW*

SWAN VILLAGE: This is the view looking down on the Great Bridge branch from Bilhay Lane bridge as a dilapidated 0-6-0PT, thought to be No 3792 of the '5700' series, heads towards West Bromwich with just a brake-van in tow. There is much to note in the scene which was taken in 1965; in the background on the extreme right can be seen a westbound freight train approaching the portal of Black Lake Tunnel, and to the right of the footbridge is the new booking hall, which had replaced the attractive timber structures some seven years earlier. Contrast the two distant signal boxes, both of which protect level crossings on Swan Lane; that on the main line is of traditional Great Western wooden construction, while that on the branch is of a more recent and robust brick design with a strengthened roof, which was a wartime measure to protect the box against bomb damage. There is a fan of goods sidings on the left and in the background can be seen a newly constructed housing estate, part of an ongoing programme to improve the nation's housing stock following the losses incurred during the war.

An industrial complex now stands on the trackbed of the branch, which has obliterated all trace of the old station, and the remaining points of reference are restricted to the two tower blocks in the background. Above the apex of the roof of the extreme right unit the upper part of the portal of Black Lake Tunnel is just visible. The Midland Metro, which follows the course of the old main line, can also be seen on the extreme right. *Eric Rogers/JW*

WEST BROMWICH is located on the south-eastern boundary of the Black Country and, like most of its neighbours, owes its growth in the 19th century to locally mined coal. However its continued prosperity was due to manufacturing and chemicals until recently, when these industries were badly hit by late-20th-century economic recessions. The town became the major intermediate location on the Birmingham, Dudley & Wolverhampton Railway when a station situated close to the town centre opened with the railway line in 1854. The town was well served by the Great Western, but probably became the biggest loser when the line was closed in 1972, joining the ranks of major towns without direct rail links. It could be argued that nearby Oldbury, whose station was later transformed into a 'parkway' and renamed Sandwell & Dudley, adequately serves the town, many will disagree. This view of the station is looking down from the bridge at the western end, as a Birmingham Snow Hill-bound Class 116 DMU awaits departure. As with other stations on the route, most of the accommodation was situated on the up platform constructed in the distinctive building style traditional for the line. The signal box governed not only the main line but also a relief line that ran behind the down platform, beyond which was a sizable goods yard. The squat tower of Trinity Church features in the background, contrasting with the new tower block on the extreme right.

The Midland Metro West Bromwich Central tram stop stands on the site of the old Great Western station and is linked to the town's central bus station, creating a transport hub. The town centre is just beyond the bus station, on the extreme left of this 29 November 2009 view as Metro tram No 02 draws to a stand with a Birmingham Snow Hill-bound working. Almost all trace of the old station has been removed, except for the wall on the right that once backed onto the rear of the down platform to keep it separate from the relief line that ran alongside. The crowd of people streaming towards the tram are not potential passengers, but worshippers from a local temple, who are taking a short-cut over the tram tracks to the town centre after prayers.
*Peter Shoesmith/JW*

WEST BROMWICH: Looking towards Wolverhampton from the up platform shows the line heading into a wide cutting; of the quadruple tracks, those on the far side are the relief and goods yard lines. Three substantial bridges carry highways over the railway, the nearest being Lyng Lane. Of equal interest is the early GWR-design railcar seen departing with a service from Birmingham Snow Hill to Dudley. This unit, No W8W, is of a design first introduced in 1934, eventually amounting to some 38 vehicles, all powered by AEC engines. The first batch was constructed by Park Royal Coachworks, but the second batch, including W8W, were products of the Gloucester Railway & Carriage Company. Later versions featured a less rounded front-end design, as well as a parcels unit and a two-car variation. The last examples survived until 1962 and three have been preserved.

The second view *(below)* from virtually the same spot dates from around 1953, and shows an experimental DMU drawing away with a down local service. It had been manufactured by the British United Traction Company (BUT) as a speculative venture at a time when the industry was looking beyond steam as a source of traction. The bodywork was produced by Park Royal, but assembled by BUT. The DMUs were powered by the same AEC engines as those used in London's 'Green Line' buses of the day. Indeed, the units were described at the time as incorporating the best features of both rail and road vehicles. However, they were noted for rough riding and had some difficulty operating track circuits, and were withdrawn in 1959. Maybe they actually incorporated the worst features of rail and road vehicles.

Midland Metro tram No 13 is virtually in the same position as it heads for Wolverhampton St George's. All three bridges remain intact and, except for some evidence of repointing and the addition of the triangular coping stones on the parapet overlooking the now electrified running lines, they have not changed much. The trackbed once occupied by the relief line and the tracks leading to the goods yard is now used as a car park and can be readily identified by the palisade fencing. *Eric Rogers/Peter Shoesmith/JW*

WEST BROMWICH: Looking at the West Bromwich of today it is difficult to envisage that for many years the cream of Great Western motive power passed through on a daily basis, and you can't get much 'creamier' than 'King' No 6001 *King Edward VII* majestically taking the curve through the station with an up express. The 'Kings' were the staple motive power on the Paddington to Birmingham and Wolverhampton trains, but because of gauging issues the class did not go any further north than the latter. Of note is the intricate ironwork on the posts supporting the platform canopy.

Lyng Lane bridge and the curvature of the track is all that remains as a reminder that this was once the route of 'Kings'! Metro tram No 06 approaches West Bromwich Central with a Birmingham Snow Hill-bound service on 29 November 2009. While it is very easy to hanker for the past, the people of West Bromwich probably now enjoy a greatly improved service than that offered by either the Great Western or the later British Railways, with peak-time Metro tram services operating every 6-8 minutes.
*Paul Dorney/JW*

WEST BROMWICH: Looking towards Birmingham Snow Hill from the down platform reveals some of the adjacent buildings looking a little the worse for wear, although it must be remembered that British towns and cities were still recovering from wartime bomb damage well into the early 1960s, and capital was being concentrated on new buildings rather than repairing life-expired domestic and commercial properties. However, the line-side hut looks to be in good order, probably used by the shunters who looked after the main goods yard on the right, and a smaller fan of sidings of the left-hand (up) side. A pannier tank of the '5700' series awaits the road from the down yard, as '4900' series 'Hall' No 4995 *Eaton Hall* approaches on a down passenger train.

The second view, again looking towards Snow Hill but from roughly halfway along the down platform, provides more detail of the up platform, particularly the canopy and standard GWR-pattern footbridge. A Class 116 DMU approaches with a local service to Wolverhampton Low Level, the unit displays in the front left-hand window its set number as allocated by Tyseley Depot. Note the loading gauge behind the wall beyond the footbridge on the up side. The tower of Trinity Church is just visible above the leading car of the DMU and the 'cool dude' on the up platform with the dark glasses dates this scene to around 1965.

Except for the original Great Western blue-brick retaining wall at the rear of the down platform and the tower of Trinity Church lurking behind the jib of a digger, there is nothing to tie in the eastern end of the Metro stop with the old station. Most of the older buildings will have been demolished when the 'West Bromwich Ringway' road was built, which now separates the Metro station and the adjacent bus interchange. The presence of the diggers and the boarded-off land on the opposite side of the tram tracks indicates that redevelopment is in progress; perhaps the view of Trinity Church will disappear forever from this viewpoint. *Paul Dorney/Peter Shoesmith/JW*

WEST BROMWICH: The bell attached to the front buffer beam immediately identifies the locomotive as No 6000 *King George V*, the doyen of the class. The bell had been presented to the Great Western on the occasion of No 6000's visit to the USA in 1927, where it featured in the centenary celebrations of the Baltimore & Ohio Railroad, and was carried with pride by the locomotive for the remainder of its career on British Railways, and indeed thereafter as a main-line-registered preserved locomotive. It hauled the first steam train on British Railways following the lifting of the infamous 'steam ban', which extended from the official last day of steam on BR in August 1968 until October 1971, when No 6000 headed a train from its then base at Hereford through to Tyseley in Birmingham. It is currently on display at the National Railway Museum at York and still carries the bell. The train is passing Trinity Church, at the eastern end of West Bromwich town centre, and is a Wolverhampton to Swindon working; this was to be the last 'King' job out of Wolverhampton, on 9 September 1962.

The imposing tower of Trinity Church still identifies the location today, as tram No 06 accelerates from Trinity Way Metro stop heading for Birmingham Snow Hill. The bridge that carries Trinity Road over the railway has been enlarged to accommodate a dual carriageway and the growth of the trees between the footpath and tram lines will eventually block this view for future generations. Closer inspection also reveals the terraced housing that formed the backdrop to the passage of the 'King' in 1962. *Eric Rogers/JW*

96

WEST BROMWICH: The gangers are working hard with the preparatory work for the re-laying of the down main line on what looks like a warm but windy summer's day. This pastoral scene belies the location, which is seen from Roebuck Lane bridge, roughly equidistant between West Bromwich station and The Hawthorns Halt, the latter so named after the nearby West Bromwich Albion football ground, which that station exclusively served on match days. Heading east towards The Hawthorns Halt is '4300' Class 'Mogul' No 5375 on a train of what looks like spent ballast for disposal.

The curve of the track is the only hint today that the location is the same. Roebuck Lane bridge now carries just a footpath, as the lane was severed by the construction of the M5 motorway, which is carried over the running lines by the solid yet totally ugly bridge. A subway, best described as unpleasant, connects the old railway bridge with the truncated Roebuck Lane. Heading for Birmingham Snow Hill and just about to pass beneath the M5 is tram No 13. *Eric Rogers/JW*

**SMETHWICK WEST:** The Great Western's 'Stourbridge Extension' diverged from the main Birmingham to Wolverhampton line at Handsworth Junction and the first station was Smethwick West. Originally it was named 'Smethwick Junction' because a spur was built to join the LNWR Stour Valley line at Galton Junction, just north of its platforms, and this connection proved useful when Stourbridge line services were transferred to Birmingham New Street following the closure of Snow Hill. The Great Western connection was retained however, albeit as a long siding as far as Handsworth cement works and an adjacent scrapyard. Although mostly used by local services, the line to Stourbridge is regularly used as a diversionary route for traffic to the South West when the direct line via the Lickey Incline is closed for engineering work. One such Class 47-hauled diverted express is seen climbing from Galton Junction and through Smethwick West.

The reopening of part of the old Great Western main line from Birmingham Snow Hill to Smethwick West ultimately spelled its doom because as a new interchange station was built a short distance to the north at Smethwick Galton Bridge,

which served both the old Great Western and the electrified Stour Valley line. However an administrative error provided a stay of execution of the closure notice, and for the next 12 months a Saturday lunchtime 'parliamentary train' operated. The station eventually closed at the end of September 1996, and subsequently the station booking hall, which was situated at road level above the cutting, and the footbridge were removed. The platforms remain in situ, albeit without any edging stones, as Class 150 DMU No 150002 is seen accelerating from its stop at Galton Bridge and across Smethwick Junction with the 1128 Stratford-upon-Avon to Great Malvern service on 29 November 2009. *Both JW*

LANGLEY GREEN is now the first station on the so-called 'Stourbridge Extension' from Galton Junction following the demise of Smethwick West, and dates back to 1867 when the final gap between the line from Stourbridge Junction to Old Hill (which had opened in two phases, in 1863 to Cradley, then 1866 onwards to Old Hill) and Galton Junction on the Birmingham to Wolverhampton Stour Valley route opened for traffic. It served an area rich in industry as well as a growing population due to its location between the Birmingham and Black Country conurbations, both of which were expanding at a significant rate in the late 19th century. The station dates from the opening of the Oldbury branch to passenger services in 1885. On 3 September 1966 a Class 116 DMU draws away from Langley Green with a service for Birmingham Snow Hill, passing the impressive ex-GWR bracket signal and signal box. The booking hall is located on the left with access from the roadway on the bridge that spans the Oldbury branch, which can be seen diverging on the right. Note too the water crane, which would soon become redundant following the elimination of steam from the West Midlands area.

It is a scene of rationalisation on 5 August 2009 with only the background block of flats providing a link with the 1966 scene. The signal box and semaphores have been swept away, with Stourbridge Junction now controlling the line including the busy level crossing to the south of the station. The booking hall has also been demolished. The scene today is by necessity more head-on due to the boundary with the road now being tree-lined. The land occupied by the branch to Oldbury is now fenced off. Passing through, non-stop is Class 150 No 150005 forming the 1605 Worcester Foregate Street to Shirley service. *Peter Shoesmith/JW*

LANGLEY GREEN: The Oldbury branch opened in 1884 for freight and 1885 for passengers. Diverging from the 'Stourbridge Extension' at Langley Green, it curved away for a distance of approximately 1.25 miles to a terminus at Oldbury Town station. It proved to be quite popular, but succumbed as a wartime economy in 1915 and never reopened. However, freight did continue with daily chemical trains to the local Albright & Wilson works. On 24 April 1986 the driver of Class 25 No 25265 has just received from the Langley Green signalman the token to proceed the short distance to the chemical works. The remains of the branch line platforms can clearly be identified; note also that there is no direct access to the branch from the main line, as the connection is from the nearby yard situated beyond the road bridge in the background.

Freight traffic continued to the chemical works until 1995, at which time the stub was closed and lifted. The scene today shows the trackbed fenced off, with nature seemingly taking over. The mainline platform has been extended, or more accurately renovated, following the closure of the signal box. The background factories clearly evident in 1986 remain, although now mostly hidden behind the abundant tree growth. Heading north is a Class 150 forming the 1623 Kidderminster to Stratford-upon-Avon service on 5 August 2009. *Both JW*

OLD HILL: Rather grubby ex-GWR '7400' series 0-6-0PT No 7418 stands in Old Hill station with a train from Dudley, consisting of just one coach, its normal consist, on 13 April 1964. This was the last day of the passenger service, hence the attention being paid to the train by the photographers, this was the last working from Dudley. The Dudley branch can be seen diverging from the main line just beyond the coach, and was controlled by Old Hill signal box, which is just in shot on the extreme left of the picture. The station is positioned on Old Hill Bank, and with a gradient as steep as 1 in 52, it still presents a fearsome obstacle for heavily laden trains to the present day. The summit is in Old Hill Tunnel, about a mile beyond the station.

There have been a number of changes at Old Hill over the intervening years, with a booking office and waiting room on the platform perhaps the most welcome, as the old facilities looked just about ready to fall down in 1964. Note also that the footbridge has been repositioned from the south end of the platform, where the branch to Dudley diverged, to the Birmingham end of the station. Today the station is served by a half-hour-interval service in each direction. On 4 December 2009 Class 150 No 150016 climbs through Old Hill with the 1015 Worcester Foregate Street to Dorridge service. *Paul Dorney/GD*

OLD HILL: Looking up the bank towards the tunnel in the early 1960s, 'Modified Hall' No 7906 *Fron Hall* coasts down the gradient with an evening local from Birmingham Snow Hill. This view is from the old footbridge, with the roof of the platform-based signal box on the right. Note the junction of the branch to Halesowen diverging on the right, just behind the water tower. The worn state of the booking office on the left-hand platform is plain to see, with particularly the roof looking to be in need of attention. However the platform itself indicates that trade is brisk with a good selection of parcels awaiting collection. A couple of the station staff are dealing with a trolley loaded with yet more parcels, and ahead of them is the station's platform-based set of scales.

The 'present' view is taken from the new footbridge, and Class 150 No 150010 has just passed the site of the junction to Halesowen while working the 1022 Shirley to Worcester Shrub Hill service on 4 December 2009. Regular passenger trains to Halesowen had ceased by 1927, but workmen's specials to the Austin Motor Works at Longbridge continued until 1958. Freight workings continued for a further 11 years before the branch closed completely. *John Dew/GD*

**OLD HILL HIGH STREET:** Old Hill's second station was at High Street, about a mile from the junction station, and one of four on the branch to Dudley, the others being Darby End, Windmill End and Baptist End. Blowers Green (or Netherton), the other station before Dudley was actually on the main line to Stourbridge. High Street was positioned on an embankment at the western end of Wrights Lane. On 15 December 1962 pannier tank No 6403 departs from the precariously positioned station with the 12.45pm Old Hill to Dudley train. Although less than two years from closure, all the stations on the branch had recently been refurbished.

The view from Wrights Lane today reveals no trace of the station, although the bridge retaining wall on the Dudley side (out of view) remains. A housing development now covers the site of the station, and the course of the line for some way in the direction of the junction. Of all the local branch lines in the area, the 'Windmill End' branch, as the Old Hill to Dudley line was officially called, suffered most from the growth of the local bus network. Locally, it was affectionately known as the 'Bumble Hole Line' after the place of that name near Windmill End. *John Dew/GD*

WITHYMOOR BASIN: A steeply graded single-line branch ran from Windmill End Junction, just a short distance to the south of Baptist End station, for roughly a mile to Withymoor Basin. The line ran through a heavily industrialised area, and consequently had numerous sidings. A large transhipment shed was positioned at the end of the branch at Withymoor Basin, which generated a good deal of traffic between railway and canal. Just before entering Withymoor Basin the line crossed Northfield Road, seen behind 0-6-0PT No 9614, which has just drawn up to the water tank for replenishment on 10 June 1965. If the water tank looks familiar, it is because it is now located on the Severn Valley Railway at its Eardington station. The provision of a footbridge reflects the fact that it was once a very busy branch.

The demise of transporting goods and materials by canal by the mid-1960s rendered Withymoor Basin redundant and the branch suffered a decline in traffic. By now known as 'Netherton Goods', the branch closed on 5 July 1965 after a life of 86 years. The course of the railway can still be traced from Northfield Road towards Baptist End, but the view into what was once Withymoor Basin is now blocked by a modern industrial unit. *Paul Dorney/JW*

BLOWERS GREEN: Originally known as 'Dudley Southside and Netherton', then more simply Blowers Green from 1921 the station was situated, as its original name implies, at the south end of Dudley Tunnel, on what was the Oxford, Worcester & Wolverhampton route, although in latter days most trains using the station were off the Old Hill line. On 12 April 1964, the day prior to the withdrawal of the passenger service to Old Hill, pannier tank No 6434 is seen propelling a Dudley to Old Hill service from Dudley Tunnel, the southern portal of which can be seen beyond the train. Blowers Green station had actually closed some two years earlier, although the branch-line trains continued to pass through. The junction for the Old Hill branch was just a few yards behind the photographer on the other side of the road bridge, as was the signal box.

The line through Blowers Green remained open after the closure of the Old Hill branch, and until 1993 still carried freight from the old South Staffordshire route from Walsall onwards to Stourbridge Junction and beyond. However, in 1993 the section of the line from Walsall to nearby Brierley Hill also closed, although at this location nature has not taken over as much as elsewhere, and the track is still clearly evident, as is the portal of the tunnel. The booking office, which was positioned at road level, also survives. There are plans for a Midland Metro extension from Wednesbury through Dudley and Blowers Green to the nearby Merry Hill Shopping Centre. The route of the old branch to Old Hill is now severed by the embankment carrying the A461 trunk road. *Peter Shoesmith/GD*

BILSTON WEST: Bilston was graced with two stations, both of Great Western origin, and not very far apart. Bilston Central was on the main line from Snow Hill to Low Level, while neighbouring Bilston West was the first station from Priestfield Junction on the line to Dudley. It opened in 1854 and survived through to the pre-Beeching withdrawal of the passenger service between Wolverhampton and Dudley as a consequence of being unable to compete both economically and practically with the local bus services. At the Wolverhampton end of the station a branch diverged to Stewarts & Lloyds Bilston Steelworks which was one of the locality's major industrial concerns. The station looks to be still very well maintained as pannier tank No 3677 departs with the 3.57pm Wolverhampton Low Level to Kidderminster local service on 28 April 1962, some three months before the withdrawal of the passenger service on 30 July.

Freight traffic continued to use the line until it finally succumbed on 1 April 1968, when the entire section from Priestfield Junction to Dudley closed. The area has seen significant redevelopment in recent years, particularly of the road network, which has resulted in all traces of Bilston West station being obliterated, except for the embankment along which the railway ran. *John Dew/GD*

PRINCES END & COSELEY: Like Bilston, Princes End was blessed with two stations. One was on the LNWR branch from Wednesbury to Bloomfield Junction on the Stour Valley line, and the other was on the Great Western's line to Dudley. The delightfully named Daisy Bank separated the GWR's Princes End & Coseley from Bilston West. Princes End adopted the additional reference to Coseley from 1936 as it sought to compete for traffic with the nearby Coseley station on the Stour Valley line, and to differentiate it from its equally close LNWR rival. It opened in 1853, ten years earlier than the LNWR's station, and its facilities were basic until the end, unlike those at Bilston West, it had a pre-cast concrete footbridge of standard design, while the platforms and waiting shelters were of wood . On 2 December 1961 ex-GWR 'Manor' 4-6-0 No 7816

*Frilsham Manor* calls with the 1.00pm Wolverhampton Low Level to Stourbridge Junction service. As the locomotive carries an 84F shedplate, which identifies it as being based at Stourbridge Junction; it seems a little extravagant to use such a locomotive on this turn, but it is likely that the local service is being used to return the 'Manor' to its home depot and avoid an unnecessary light engine move.

As for today, the picture says it all. The station was situated in a shallow cutting that is now so overgrown that if any remnant remained it would stay hidden beneath the foliage. Suffice to say that, like Bilston West, the station closed on 30 July 1962. *John Dew/GD*

# Kingswinford branch

TETTENHALL: The purpose of the Kingswinford branch was to provide a relief line around Wolverhampton to ease congestion on the Birmingham Snow Hill main line. It opened in 1925, quite late in terms of local railway development, and ran from a junction at Oxley (near the current carriage depot) on the Wolverhampton to Shrewsbury line through to the Oxford, Worcester & Wolverhampton line at Brettell Lane, north of Stourbridge. The route had been authorised as early as 1905, but its construction was delayed, in no small measure due to the First World War. For its first seven years of operation it enjoyed a passenger service, which did not prove to be popular and was withdrawn in 1932. Freight services continued until 24 June 1965, when the line was closed. Tettenhall, a leafy and affluent suburb of Wolverhampton, was the most northerly station. It was active for just the seven years of passenger operation, but the buildings survived, as evidenced by this scene on 14 June 1957 as Churchward 2-8-0 No 2850 drifts through the station with a short southbound freight. The station is in remarkably good condition considering it has been closed for 25 years, with particularly the roof looking weather-tight and even the modesty board protecting the gentlemen's toilets still intact.

Considering that the passenger service was withdrawn in 1932 and the last freight service ran on 24 June 1965, the one compelling feature of the location today is the survival of the original booking hall, complete with canopy and part of the down platform, all in excellent condition. Wolverhampton City

Council has funded a restoration project, and the station is now used as a field station for the surrounding Smestow Valley Local Nature Reserve, which includes part of the trackbed within its boundary. A walkway now follows the trackbed, bringing a touch of rural delight to the centre of an urbanised area. Both platforms remain in situ, while the goods yard, which was situated behind the station, is now a car park. The goods shed survives, in good condition and still in commercial use. The location is well worth a visit. *Geoff Bannister/JW*

WOMBOURN: The only other significant station on the Kingswinford branch was at Wombourn (the railway omitted the final 'e' of Wombourne), which for a short while was known as 'The Bratch', after a nearby stream. This too enjoyed only seven years of life as a passenger station, from 1925 until 1932. A booking hall was provided on the up side, with a smaller waiting room on the opposite down platform. The roof of the signal box is just evident above the second coach of a Wolverhampton Low level to Henley-on-Thames ECS working hauled by ex-GWR '4900' Class 4-6-0 No 6910 *Gossington Hall* on 17 August 1957; the train had earlier worked north on a summer Saturday holiday train from Bournemouth Central to Wolverhampton Low Level. A large water tower was also provided, the tank of which is just visible to the left of the down waiting room roof. While the station buildings have survived well, the same cannot be said for the platforms, which have been severely cut back.

Amazingly, the old booking hall survives today in very good condition and, as with Tettenhall, has retained its canopy. The restoration has been undertaken in a careful manner, the only noticeable change, other than the fencing along the platform edge, being that the brickwork on the far chimney has been improved and strengthened. Restoration of the southbound platform has also been undertaken, but the only trace of the northbound platform is the raised earthwork beside the trackbed; the waiting room, water tower and signal box have long since been removed. Today the trackbed forms part of the South Staffordshire Railway Walk, while part of the old booking hall is used as a café catering for passing ramblers. This is one route that will never see trains again, so it is nice to see the course of the line being put to good use. *Geoff Bannister/JW*

# Trent Valley line

TAMWORTH LOW LEVEL: The Trent Valley route from Rugby to Stafford was conceived as a means of bypassing the bottleneck of Birmingham and the Black Country for through workings between Euston and the North West of England and Scotland. As such it became probably the most strategic route passing through Staffordshire, but other than easing congestion did not bring great prosperity to the towns and city along the route as most trains, especially today, tend to speed through non-stop. The route passes from Warwickshire to Staffordshire just to the east of Tamworth, which became the major railhead on the line due to the growth of postal traffic, with up to 2,000 mail sacks being processed between the two routes in any one day; such mail trains no longer operate. Charging through on the up main on 21 June 1959 is rebuilt 'Royal Scot' 4-6-0 No 46139 *The Welch Regiment* at the head of the up 'Ulster Express'. Tamworth was the point where the four-track formation from Nuneaton was reduced to double track for the climb to Hademore troughs and Lichfield. At the western end of the station Tamworth Low Level signal box controlled the end of the double-track section as well as the chord line that then connected the low-level and high-level lines. Just above the water crane next to the up fast can be seen the roof of the High Level signal box.

Except for the addition of the overhead electrification masts and wiring, Tamworth changed little until the advent of the Trent Valley quadrupling scheme. Here at the east end of the station everything remains in roughly the same place, albeit upgraded. The High Level platforms have been rebuilt, and the height of the bridge increased to cater for overhead electrification. The staircases between the two sets of platforms have also been rebuilt in brick instead of wood, and new lifts installed, replacing those used for the mail traffic. However, at the other end the four-track formation now continues to the west. The resultant resignalling resulted in the closure of Tamworth Low Level signal box in 2008, with responsibility for the line passing to a new panel in Rugby. On 12 December 2009 a Virgin Class 390 'Pendolino' speeds through Low Level with a Euston-bound service. *Michael Mensing/JW*

TAMWORTH LOW LEVEL: The original four-track alignment is shown to good effect in this 8 March 1958 scene as an unidentified 'Jubilee' restarts a southbound excursion from the up platform. Note the array of semaphore signals in the distance, but which box controls them is a matter of debate as the signal box on the right is shorn of its nameplate and looks to have closed, although the actual date so far has defied detection. Note that the chef in the Kitchen Car seems to be having a short break from his duties, and is watching a couple of individuals around the parapet of the bridge that carries the line over the River Tame. Dominating the left-hand side is the large, squat pump house, for so long a feature of the station.

A Virgin Class 390 'Pendolino' hurries through Tamworth on 13 December 2009 with a northbound express. The basic layout to the east has changed little compared with the radical track alterations at the western end of the station. The signal box has been removed and, most noticeably, the pump house has been demolished. *Michael Mensing/JW*

LICHFIELD TRENT VALLEY: The A38 Lichfield bypass was completed in 1972, so has always crossed electrified lines. This is the scene pre-'TV4' looking south towards Hademore, and records the final outing of AC electric Class 87s for Virgin Trains. The class had been the staple motive power on West Coast trains since their introduction in 1974 and had put in sterling service. On 10 June 2005 Nos 87010 *Driver Tommy Farr* and 87002 *AC Locomotive Group* (carrying Porterbrook livery) head north on their final Virgin diagram from Euston to Manchester Piccadilly, this was a one-way working. The class did later feature on temporary locomotive-hauled diagrams on the Birmingham route due to the need to withdraw members of Virgin's 'Pendolino' fleet for rectification work. The scene here had not altered from the date the bridge was installed, but all was soon to change.

'TV4', the four-tracking of the previous double-track section of the Trent Valley route from Tamworth via Lichfield to Armitage was part of a greater West Coast upgrade with a view to increasing both line speeds and train movements throughout between Euston and Glasgow, which could be fully exploited by Virgin Trains' new fleet of 140mph tilting 'Pendolinos'. At this point the existing reinforced concrete road bridge had to be widened to accommodate the extra two running lines, and was one of the biggest civil engineering tasks of 'TV4'.

Also the line south towards Hademore ran along a shallow embankment that also had to be widened, and the opportunity was taken to slightly ease the reverse curve. New and extended overhead structures plus the now mandatory gantry to carry signalling combine to create a completely different scene. With some infrastructure work remaining, but with the new quadruple track fully operational, a Virgin Class 390 'Pendolino' races north during the summer of 2008. The sadness is that due to cost issues the line was upgraded for 125mph running rather than the projected 140mph. *Both JW*

LICHFIELD TRENT VALLEY is seen again in this tranquil scene on 2 December 1961 as Stanier Class 8F No 48258 trundles north with a Harts Hill (near Nuneaton) to Stafford ballast train. Note the long winding curve at this point and the contrast between the 'old' railway, with the line of telegraph poles, and the 'new' railway, as evidenced by the posts that will eventually form part of the overhead electrification of the line. Out of view on the left stands the bracket signal that governs access to the station loop. The train is about to pass beneath the 'old' Burton Road bridge, which is situated at the eastern end of Lichfield Trent Valley station.

The basic layout remained with the original electrification scheme, and it was only with 'TV4' that the formation was greatly opened out. Gradually the south side of the line was developed and is now a large industrial and retail park, while the background vista changed significantly with the completion of the A38 Lichfield eastern bypass, which can seen on the distant embankment. The curvature remains quite tight, but does not inhibit the Virgin 'Pendolino' fleet, which reach virtually maximum tilt when running through Lichfield at line speed. The West Coast is also a busy freight route, especially at night. However, there are also many daytime trains, one such flow being the Freightliners from Felixstowe to terminals in the North West of England and Scotland. On 7 April 2008 Class 90 No 90042 approaches Lichfield with a well-laden working for Ditton, on Merseyside. *Roger Shenton/JW*

LICHFIELD TRENT VALLEY: Looking down into the station on 4 July 1953 from the 'new' Burton Road bridge, we see 'Princess Coronation' 4-6-2 No 46252 *City of Leicester* sweeping north with the down 'Royal Scot'. In the background is Lichfield High Level on the LNWR's route from Walsall to Wichnor Junction. The High Level station was seriously damaged by fire in the late 1950s and closed in 1965 with the withdrawal of passenger services between Walsall and Burton-upon-Trent. On the left can be seen the chord running up from the Trent Valley to the higher route, while on the extreme left is the siding running into Lichfield Maltings. On the right is a cattle dock, for many years a favourite place for trainspotters to watch the passing trains. Low Level was the scene of a serious accident on 1 January 1946 when, due to a points failure, a fish train was diverted into the up platform loop and collided with a stationary passenger train.

The scene today is much cluttered by the overhead electrification masts and wiring. 'TV4' has not affected the station area particularly, but of course the four-track alignment is now continuous and incorporates what were the up and down platform loops. Lichfield Low Level signal box, for so long a feature of the station due to its prominent position between the up and down running lines, closed and was removed in June 2008 when signalling for the route passed to the new Rugby panel. Both up and down platforms have been extended to cater for longer trains, the latter across the site of the cattle dock. On the left is the chord to the Wichnor Junction line, controlled at High Level by the last manual signal box in the area. The High Level station reopened in 1988 when Cross City line services were extended from nearby Lichfield City, and a Class 323 EMU can be seen awaiting departure with a Cross City line train to Birmingham New Street and beyond. A northbound Virgin Class 390 'Pendolino' tilts through the station; the exposed drawbar equipment suggests that the unit has been subject to a recent locomotive-hauled drag. It is interesting to note that the chord between the two routes is not electrified, and the High Level wiring stops at the platform end of that station, some distance short of the junction. *Peter Shoesmith/JW*

LICHFIELD TRENT VALLEY: This pre-electrification view looking north from the 'new' Burton Road bridge reveals on the extreme left the surviving original station building; this dates back to the opening of the Rugby to Stafford line in 1847, but was replaced by two new stations just to the south, which jointly served the Trent Valley and South Staffordshire lines. In the distance is Lichfield No 2 signal box and on the right is a goods yard. Note the connection from the Lichfield chord line at Trent Valley High level Junction which crosses the formation from right to left. Judging by the brightness of the ballast there has been some recent relaying on the up fast. Standing on the up slow awaiting the road is ex-WD 2-8-0 No 90150 on a short freight.

Originally the platform loops extended to the west of the station to a point where the line entered a cutting. 'TV4' resulted in the cutting being opened out to accommodate the new four-track formation, which included the rebuilding of an occupation bridge at the neck of the cutting. The engineer's sidings on the up (right-hand) side have been remodelled, and the connection to the chord to High Level is now an extended 'ladder' type crossing that reaches the down slow lines at a point just beyond the enlarged occupation bridge. The old station building was demolished in the 1970s. A Virgin Class 390 'Pendolino' speeds towards the tight curve at Trent Valley station, which will necessitate full-tilt in order to pass comfortably through. *David C. Williams/JW*

115

LICHFIELD TRENT VALLEY: The Lichfield chord provides a north-to-west connection from the upper, former South Staffordshire line down to the Trent Valley route. It is regarded as being a freight connection, and is not wired. Lichfield Trent Valley High Level Junction signal box is situated at the summit of the chord, and controls just the top junction, while the Low Level connection is now under the new Rugby panel. From a traffic perspective it does provide alternative options for traffic from Derby to Crewe should the North Staffordshire route via Uttoxeter be unavailable. On 19 March 1960 Fowler Class 4F No 44599 gently descends from the High Level Junction with a ballast train bound for Rugeley. Of interest is the non-standard tender, and the ballast ploughs fitted to the brake-van. In the background are the substantial maltings buildings belonging to J. & C. H. Evans & Co Ltd.

The scene today is viewed from Platform 1 at Low Level, the chord line is behind the stonework constructed in 1987 identifying the station and advising that it is 285 miles from Glasgow and 116 from London Euston. The chord continues to see traffic, but in recent years that has not amounted to many trains. Currently there is one regular booked daytime freight, and it is visited by the Network Rail Track Monitoring train when it is scheduled for its weekly check of the West Coast Main Line to London Euston. The maltings have long been demolished, and the industrial unit that now occupies the site is also closed. *Roger Shenton/ JW*

LICHFIELD TRENT VALLEY: The premises of Rom Ltd are situated next to the down lines at Lichfield, just to the north of the station, and the works were rail-connected in 1963. The exchange sidings were situated behind the original Lichfield Trent Valley station, which can be seen of the right-hand side of this late-1960s scene in which an early LMR AC electric locomotive can be seen at the head of a rake of mineral wagons about to proceed north towards Stafford. Rom Ltd specialises in reinforcement products, and the consist of the train may well contain the scrap by-products of Rom's production process. For a period of time Rom had its own works shunter which was an early diesel locomotive built by Kerr, Stuart of Stoke-on-Trent in 1929, and subsequently rebuilt in 1959; it ended its commercial life at Rom's Lichfield site, and is now preserved at the Foxfield Railway.

The plant remained rail-connected until 1988, and the area where the sidings once lay is now hardstanding for one of Rom's major product lines, the panels of steel rodding used in reinforced concrete, piles of which can be seen stored around the site. The only remaining feature is the high-roofed building in the background, through which Rom's internal rail system once ran. The old Lichfield station building has also been demolished, the electrification masts pinpointing its location. *Peter Shoesmith/JW*

ELMHURST, NEAR LICHFIELD: Near the village of Elmhurst, on the western periphery of Lichfield, the Trent Valley line passes beneath the A515 Kings Bromley road, where Ex-LMS 'Jubilee' 4-6-0 No 45580 *Burma* is seen heading north along the easy grades at this point with the 1.25pm Euston to Blackpool and Perth express on 22 September 1959. In the background is Elmhurst Level Crossing signal box.

The location today is still a gentle rural setting, but the railway has changed beyond all recognition. Virgin Class 390 'Pendolino' No 390040 charges north with a Euston to Liverpool Lime Street express on 4 December 2009, running on what was until not so long ago the up fast line which, following the quadrupling, is now the down fast. The 'new' railway on the left – the extra tracks laid as part of 'TV4' – can be clearly identified by the clean ballast. European legislation now insists that all lineside signalling is carried on overhead gantries, hence the structure now spanning all the running lines. *Roger Shenton/JW*

RUGELEY TRENT VALLEY: 'TV4' covered the gap in quadruple tracks between Tamworth and Armitage; at the latter it joined up with the existing four-tracked formation that continues via Rugeley to Colwich Junction, where the line to Stoke-on-Trent and Manchester diverges. From Colwich the Trent Valley line continues as double track through Shugborough Tunnel before again opening out into a four-track alignment at Milford through to Stafford and beyond. From the footbridge at Rugeley Trent Valley a unidentified Class 7F 0-8-0 plods past Rugeley No 2 signal box on the up fast with a rake of assorted wagons. A goods yard is located behind the signal box, while on the extreme left is the Cannock Chase line, which joins the Trent Valley at this point.

From the steps of the same footbridge, a Virgin Class 390 'Pendolino' is seen heading south at roughly the same spot as the freight in the earlier scene. The signal box was abolished with the inauguration of the electrification scheme in 1967, and the yard beyond is now used by the engineer's department. The Cannock Chase connection remains, although the passenger service, which until recently ran through to Stafford, now terminates at Rugeley Trent Valley. This is mainly as a result of an enhanced and regular-interval Trent Valley stopping service, which commenced in 2008. The Trent Valley was all about speed and convenience, and in the past the towns and city on its route suffered a very poor service; 'TV4' provided the track capacity, and now arguably the route has its best local service ever! *Eric Rogers/JW*

# Other railways

ESSINGTON: A system of mineral lines ran through the village of Essington, where a number of pits had been established. One of the lines was from Hilton Main Colliery, situated near to Featherstone on the outskirts of Wolverhampton, and ran via Holly Bank Colliery in Essington to a canal wharf at Short Heath near Willenhall. One of its most endearing features was a unique signal box, attached to the corner of what was once the Holly Bank Colliery Company's wages office and truck shop building, which controlled a level crossing over Bursnips Road in Essington. This line closed in 1965, but not before a bridge over the nearby M6 had been provided for during the construction of the motorway. On 27 March 1964 a Yorkshire Engine Co 0-6-0 diesel shunter is seen crossing Bursnips Road and heading for Holly Bank. The wagons in the background indicate the position now occupied by the bridge over the M6.

It is good to see that the signal box has survived. The whole building has been renovated to a high standard and is now an attractive residential property with the old signal box incorporated into the redesign – having seen the finished product, it was worth it. And, as an Essington lad, it was a happy reminder of times past! *Peter Shoesmith/JW*

THE CHASEWATER LIGHT RAILWAY began life as the 'Railway Preservation Society West Midlands District', whose inaugural meeting was back in 1959. Its first location was in Hednesford, before moving to a site at Chasewater, where a man-made lake had been established in 1770 to service the local canal network, by the 1980s it was being developed as a recreational attraction. The railway had acquired a collection of mainly industrial locomotives and operated public trains for a period on a short stretch of track that was once part of the Midland Railway route from Aldridge to Brownhills, which led into a web of line serving collieries in the vicinity. However the railway was finding life difficult, but a solution was near at hand, and from an entirely unlikely source. The 'past' picture reflects the location of the original site at Chasewater, which today is buried beneath the M6 Toll Road.

The coming of the Toll Road was to have a profound effect on the railway. Firstly a compensation package for the loss of its original site was sufficient to fund the move a short distance to the north and construct a sizeable station now known as Brownhills West. Once the momentum started it was maintained as the line was extended first around Chasewater Lake to a new station at Chasewater Heaths, then finally to a new platform at its eastern terminus, Chasetown Church Street. In the meantime grants had been obtained for the construction of a new three-road engine shed and workshop, and the locomotive fleet was increased, so now the railway was on a completely different but stronger footing. Regular advertised services now operate, such as this 'Santa Special' seen departing from Brownhills West on 6 December 2009 hauled by Bagnall 0-4-0ST No 2648 of 1940, named *Linda*. The new station building, which contains a shop and restaurant facilities, can be seen just behind the train, while the gabled roof of the engine shed is just visible over the various stock items on the right. The signal box is from Madeley Junction, and is being installed to govern all movements around the station area and yard. These are not true 'past and present' images in the accepted sense of this book, as they relate to different sites, albeit not far apart, but actually describe the more profound story of the 'past and present' of the Chasewater Light Railway perhaps better than any words. *Both JW*

CHASEWATER NCB: The Midland line from Aldridge through Brownhills joined the Cannock Chase & Wolverhampton Railway near Norton Canes, and the latter then curved around Chasewater Lake via Chasetown to join the LNWR's Walsall to Lichfield line at Anglesey Sidings. This line followed an alignment very close to the existing course of the present Chasewater Light Railway, and this scene is just a short distance from the latter's terminus at Chasetown Church Road. It is in the vicinity of Cannock Chase No 2 Pit and the 0-6-0ST 'Austerity' locomotive (No 3789 of 1953) appears to be propelling the rake of wagons towards the colliery sidings on 27 March 1959.

The area has seen substantial redevelopment of late, including new roads that pass through the site, mainly as a spin-off from the building of the M6 Toll Road. However, the derelict house surrounded by the palisade fence seen through the gap in the trees on the right is the same one that can be seen on the right of the 'past' scene. The line closed in 1962. *Peter Shoesmith/JW*

CHASETOWN ENGINE SHED: A locomotive depot was provided at Chasetown consisting of three roads beneath an all-over gabled roof. It was situated near the end of Church Street in Chasetown, and close to the current terminus of the Chasewater Light Railway. On 6 March 1960 the shed is occupied by Robert Stephenson & Hawthorns No 7106 of 1943, and two Hunslet 'Austerities', Nos 3772 of 1952 and 3789 of 1953. The engine shed will have closed in 1962 together with the branch.

The location today corresponds roughly with the clubhouse of Burntwood Rugby Football Club, which is the building beyond the touch line of the rugby pitch. The rugby ground is situated at the end of Church Street and the terminus of the Chasewater Light Railway is situated just beyond the wall to the right of the clubhouse. *J. A. Pedon, Chasewater Light Railway collection/JW*

LITTLETON COLLIERY was the last working pit on the Cannock Chase coalfield, and survived until 1993. The first shafts were sunk in 1872 but flooding caused work to be suspended, and it was more than 20 years later in 1899, after two years of further work, that the mine was formally registered. It had an extensive internal railway system, including a branch of some 2.5 miles to exchange sidings with BR at Penkridge. This view shows part of the system that ran parallel to the main A34 Cannock to Stafford trunk road, and illustrates Hunslet 'Austerity' No 1752 of 1943 in the process of shunting wagons containing domestic coal, judging by the presence of a coal merchant's wagon on the extreme left. The date is recorded as 27 March 1970, some 18 months after the end of main-line BR steam operation.

Following closure the site of the colliery was cleared and only now is in the course of redevelopment. A new community centre occupies part of the site, while some land facing the A34 has been grassed over, and a new housing development has been built on the remaining site. However, despite the profusion of silver birch trees and some landscaping, the location of the earlier scene is identified by the terraced houses that remain today. To the right, the land that was previously meadows has now been taken up for residential use. *Peter Shoesmith/JW*

# Midland from Tamworth to Burton-upon-Trent

TAMWORTH HIGH LEVEL is where the Midland main line from Birmingham to Derby crosses the Trent Valley line at right angles. High Level was the first station, opened in 1839 by the Birmingham & Derby Railway. A chord, similar to that still in situ at Lichfield Trent Valley today, climbed from the Trent Valley up slow line to the Midland's up line. A plan for a similar chord running from north to east was never built. The Trent Valley platforms opened in 1847 and the station became a key interchange point for the Royal Mail's postal trains. High Level was a narrow site, and it was necessary to locate the signal box behind the up platform with the cabin extended over the platform. On 15 June 1963 'Jubilee' 4-6-0 No 45690 *Leander* arrives at the head of a Newcastle to Bristol train. The locomotive is now preserved, and currently has a main-line operating certificate.

The general layout at High Level has changed little, except that the lifts, staircases and waiting rooms have been modernised. The signal box closed when control of the area was taken over by the new Saltley panel, but its location can still be clearly identified by the break in the concrete wall where the steps to the box were once positioned. The postal traffic, once so important for the station, has ceased, but in recent years the growth of passenger traffic has been significant, especially on the cross-country route. One such service, from Nottingham to Cardiff, in the hands of Class 170 No 170107, draws into the station on 15 December 2009. *David C. Williams/JW*

WICHNOR JUNCTION is where the ex-LNWR South Staffordshire route from Walsall and Lichfield joins the Midland main line from Birmingham to Derby. Both routes approach the junction from the south across low viaducts carrying the lines over the River Trent. Originally, as each line was owned by a different company, a raft of exchange sidings was provided on the up side. The signal box seen here, on the down side of the line, was the fourth, and dates back to 1953; it survived until 1969. A down loop ran behind the signal box, which was later truncated into a siding with the removal of the connection at the Burton-upon-Trent end. Approaching the main lines from the Lichfield direction on 10 August 1959 is Fowler Class 4F 0-6-0 No 44605 hauling 0-6-0 diesel shunter No 12095 and a brake-van. The diesel shunter was allocated to Aston shed, and had been built in Derby where it was probably being taken for overhaul or repair. This view was taken from a level crossing that carried a farm track across the railway.

The location today, especially for enthusiasts, is more commonly known as Catholme. A bridge now carries the farm track over the line at this point; road traffic increased when a gravel extraction plant was established next to the railway on the Burton-upon-Trent side of the bridge. The site of the signal box is just below the bridge, and the location of the sidings on both sides of the main running lines can clearly be identified from the shape of the land within the railway fence. Wichnor Junction itself is now sited nearer the viaducts, and is of the 'ladder' type, it can just be seen in the background with the Lichfield line diverging to the south-west. On 12 December 2009 DBS Class 66 No 66204 leads classmate No 66013 on a northbound light-engine move through Catholme. *David C. Williams/JW*

WICHNOR JUNCTION: The boards of the old level crossing can just be seen in the bottom left-hand corner, as BR Class 9F 2-10-0 No 92086 works south on an empty stock working on 7 August 1959, probably in connection with a Summer Saturday holiday express working the following day. Although designed as a heavy-haul freight locomotive the class did see a fair amount of passenger work. The loop line, which ran behind the signal box, was still in situ at this time and the bracket signal covered the loop, main line and Lichfield route.

The same view today provides not quite the rural feel of the previous picture. The course of the loop can clearly be identified in the foreground as Fastline Class 66/3 No 66301 passes with a loaded 'merry-go-round' coal train for Ironbridge Power Station on 12 December 2009. In the background can be seen the giant Argos Distribution Centre which is fed by regular intermodal services to Burton-upon-Trent, with the containers being ferried to Argos by road. Additionally, hidden behind the coal train, is the Central Rivers Bombardier Maintenance Depot, built to maintain the then fleet of Virgin Class 220 and 221 'Voyagers', which were purchased to cover cross-country services. This facility remains (although the Cross Country franchise is now with Arriva Trains). The depot is affectionately known locally as 'Muddy Waters'. *David C. Williams/JW*

# Burton-upon-Trent 1

Burton-upon-Trent has at least a 400-year association with brewing, which remains the town's major industry today. The number of breweries has reduced, mainly by amalgamation, but the association of the town with brewing remains as strong as ever. Its location on the River Trent is ideal, both for water extraction and, in earlier days, for transportation. The railways were to revolutionise the brewing industry, as virtually at a stroke they opened up markets hitherto unavailable for no other reason than distance. With the town occupying a prime position on the Birmingham & Derby Railway (B&DR), which opened in 1839, it immediately had easy access to Birmingham and, via a connection at Hampton in Arden, to London via the London & Birmingham Railway. Eventually the B&DR was absorbed by the Midland Railway whose subsequent growth further served to expand the markets for Burton's ales. The railways of Burton also extended into virtually every corner of the town, as the breweries used rail up to as recently as the 1970s to both import raw materials and export the finished product.

BURTON-UPON-TRENT: In 1883 a new station was opened at Burton, slightly to the south of its predecessor, which had evolved over the years since the line opened in 1839. It was a magnificent building, befitting the growing importance of the town, and consisted of a substantial island platform, both long and wide, which had both platform and through roads to maximise operating flexibility. Bay platforms were provided at each end for local terminating services. The platform actually extended beneath the roadway at the Derby end, making it difficult in one glance to get a true idea of the substance of the place. An eye-catching half-timbered construction with a high gabled roof was located roughly halfway along the platform, which housed both refreshment rooms and offices. The main entrance was at road level, with a large canopied portico from the main carriageway. In August 1964 Fowler Class 4 0-6-0 No 44034 arrives with an early evening train from Leicester, which will have travelled via Coalville and gained access to the Midland line at Leicester Junction, part of a triangle situated less than a mile to the south of Leicester Midland station. Burton Station South signal box can be seen in the distance.

It is difficult to believe today that such an attractive building, arguably a major asset to any location, could be demolished. But demolished it was, the task being undertaken in 1971. This scene (*opposite top*) shows the station in its final days, shorn of its canopies as 'Peak' Type 4 No 23 eases to a stand with a northbound cross-country express on 9 April 1971. Note that colour light signalling is now in place.

The replacement for the grand old station is seen in the third picture: the most basic of buildings totally devoid of any design flair. In fact it is a statement of defeat: the railways were in freefall decline in the 1970s, when talk of closures and rationalisation was rife and any spark of enterprise was quickly extinguished. Maybe an overly pessimistic view, but looking at the result at Burton the question must be, why was it allowed to happen? A building such as the old station would surely have been listed nowadays. The good news is that, with the growth of both cross-country and local traffic, Burton is again a busy station, with alternate Cross Country services stopping at either Tamworth or Burton. On 8 December a non-stop Class 220 'Voyager' speeds through with northbound working. *Phil Waterfield/Peter Shoesmith/JW*

**BURTON-UPON-TRENT, WETMORE SIDINGS:** Wetmore, on the northern edge of Burton, was an interesting place if for no other reason than it was where lines from four railway companies came together. Perhaps the most unlikely was the Great Northern which accessed the area via its line from Derby and Eggington Junction, and reached Burton by means of running rights over the North Staffordshire line from Stoke-on-Trent. An example of the GNR's presence is 'K1' 2-6-0 No 62010 blasting off the Great Northern branch and onto the bridge that carried the NSR branch over the Midland main line with a southbound freight which has probably brought in hops from the eastern counties.

Looking back towards the NSR bridge, which is partially hidden by the footbridge from which the previous picture was taken, we see Wetmore Sidings signal box on the right as 'Crosti'-boilered Class 9F 2-10-0 No 92027 crosses from the sidings on the down side with a short freight. Note the steeple of the long-demolished Trinity Church directly above the locomotive's tender.

The third view is looking down the main line in the early 1980s, and shows that the footbridge and NSR bridge remain, although the branch was long closed. Wetmore Sidings can be seen fanning out beyond the bridge and it is on the left-hand (down) side that an LNWR branch accessed the main line via running rights over Midland metals. Note the large bonded warehouse on the right, one of many dotted throughout the town. Passing Wetmore Sidings signal box is a Class 47 locomotive at the head of a northbound cross-country service.

In the fourth photograph it is all change at Wetmore Sidings. The signal box has been abolished, but the most significant feature is that a new road bridge stands where the old North Staffordshire line crossed the Midland. also gone is the footbridge. In the background on the left can be seen new silos that pinpoint the vast Coors' brewery, while on the right the bonded warehouse seen earlier has now acquired the legend 'Marstons Pedigree'; Marstons is now the other major brewer in Burton-upon-Trent. Heading for Nottingham is Class 170 No 170108 with a cross-country service from Cardiff on 8 December 2009. *Phil Waterfield*

**(2)/JW (2)**
**BURTON-UPON-TRENT, BOND END BRANCH:** This line commenced at Wellington Street Junction on the Shobnall branch, then dived beneath the Midland main line to emerge at Dale Street; this controlled access to a raft of sidings belonging to Worthington & Peaches Maltings, which ran down to Leicester Junction. 'Jinty' No 47629 has just emerged from the 'Bridge Hole' with a train from Shobnall, and will reverse into the Worthington & Peaches sidings after having negotiated Dale Street level crossing. Burton Station South signal box, Ind Coope's Bottling Stores and the tower of St Paul's Church are all visible on the right. A short LNWR branch also diverged at Dale Street and ran northwards to Moor Street Wharf, which was situated to the right of the 'Bridge Hole'. No 47629 finished its days at Williamthorpe Colliery as one of the last three working members of the class.

The location of the 'Bridge Hole' is now beneath a new road bridge that spans the southern throat of Burton station, and is part of a new town bypass scheme. Everard Way, which continues east from this location, follows the line of the Bond Street branch, which itself was built on filled-in land that was once the Burton Canal. If you look very carefully between the trees to the right of the white van, the tower of St Paul's Church can be seen peeking over the gables of the Ind Coope plant. *Phil Waterfield/GD*

BURTON-UPON-TRENT, BOND END BRANCH: There is a wealth of memorabilia in this scene as ex-LMS Kitson-designed Class 0F 0-4-0ST No 47000 trundles across Uxbridge Street level crossing on the Bond End branch. It appears to be both pushing and pulling as it heads towards Dale Street. Just beyond this point to the east, at Uxbridge Street Junction, branches diverged to Duke Street and New Street to the north, and Charrington Maltings to the south. Uxbridge Street signal box is tucked in on the extreme right beyond the Esso sign. No prizes either for spotting equally iconic (if you are the right age) signs for Esso Blue Paraffin, Spratts Dog Food and Persil!

Everard Way now follows the course of the Bond End branch, and the location can be pinpointed by the white gabled property on the left-hand side of Uxbridge Street. The Bond End branch beyond Uxbridge Junction closed in 1964, and the remaining lines had all finished by 1968. *Phil Waterfield/GD*

133

BURTON-UPON-TRENT, BOND END BRANCH: Just prior to Bond End itself, a further level crossing was located at the junction of Branston Road and Lichfield Street. On 2 March 1964 BR 0-4-0DH shunting locomotive No D2859 hauls the last train off the branch over the Branston Road level crossing. The entrance to the wharf is alongside the signal box, which dates back to 1902. On the other side of the road is an impressive building belonging to the Midland Joinery Works Ltd. For further nostalgia note the impressive Humber car waiting at the gates; this was an up-market marque that became part of the Rootes Group, which later, through other amalgamations, ended as part of the French-owned Peugeot company.

The location today is a very busy part of the town with a retail park and a branch of Tesco all nearby. Everard Way meets Branston Road and Lichfield Street at a frequently congested traffic island. All this development in recent years has swept away any remaining connections with the railway, but the rather gnarled tree does bear a striking resemblance to that in the scene of more than 40 years earlier – it would be nice to think they are one and the same. *Phil Waterfield/GD*

BURTON-UPON-TRENT, HAY BRANCH: The Hay branch together with the Guild Street branch, formed a circle off the main line. The former diverged virtually opposite North Stafford Junction and ran via a wharf alongside the River Trent to Hay Sidings, where the latter continued on to rejoin the main line by Horninglow Junction signal box. The area within was mainly Bass territory. On 22 July 1966 0-6-0T 'Jinty' No 47643 heads alongside the River Trent on the Hay branch at the head of nine empty mineral wagons. Ahead of the train on the left are the former Burton Brewery Company's maltings and Salt's ale stores. Note the improved flood defences.

A residential estate now occupies the site, and there is evidence that the river defences have been further improved. The branch was progressively closed down during the 1960s as the breweries increasingly looked to road haulage for their transport needs. The last train on the Hay branch is reported to have operated on 1 March 1969, carrying coal for the nearby gasworks that was situated on a short siding trailing off the branch, it was sandwiched between the Trent, the Hay branch and Wetmore Road. *Phil Waterfield/GD*

BURTON-UPON-TRENT, HAY BRANCH: Anderstaff Lane level crossing actually spanned Wetmore Road and carried the Hay branch from the main line down to the wharf. This was the third signal box to occupy the site and dated back to 1904. The original had opened in 1867, and was replaced in 1881. The background double-gabled building is the Bass Anderstaff Lane Maltings and Ale Store, while tucked in behind the signal box is the cooperage building of the former Burton's Brewery. On the footplate of No 47643 the engineman seems to be taking notice of the very smart Lancia car that is halted at the gates. The train is the same rake of mineral wagons seen previously on the Hay branch at Trent Wharf.

The signal box closed on 1 March 1969 and no trace of either it or the railway remains, and while the maltings have survived the ale store and cooperage buildings have gone. Wetmore Road remains a major thoroughfare along the eastern flank of the town. *Phil Waterfield/JW*

BURTON ON TRENT, BASS BREWERIES: The Bass breweries were situated to the south of the bridge over the Trent, with an associated fan of sidings that occupied a substantial amount of land. This view shows the sidings in their later years of operation; an unidentified Hawthorn Leslie 0-4-0ST stands at the head of a rake of assorted wagons and vans in front what was Allsopp's Old Brewery. Note the crossover in the foreground; this leads to the Guild Street branch, which is tucked away in the gap between the end of the gabled building behind the first van of the train, and the smaller building to the left. The water tower on the extreme left pinpoints the location of Bass's old brewery.

The breweries have gone, and the entire area is being redeveloped except for one important landmark – the water tower. *Peter Shoesmith/JW*

**BURTON-UPON-TRENT, HORNINGLOW (DERBY ROAD) LEVEL CROSSING:** It is easy to be confused with the name Horninglow when writing about Burton-upon-Trent, because a branch (see later) and a station on a different line share the same name. Horninglow station was situated on the Derby Road (which ran parallel to the main line from Burton town centre and was the main road out of town to the north) and on the North Staffordshire route to Uttoxeter and Stoke-on-Trent. Derby Road and the NSR intersected at a level crossing next to Horninglow station. In the mid-1960s Stanier Class 8F 2-8-0 No 48552 is doing a good job in holding up the traffic as it clanks west over the crossing and approaches Horninglow signal box and the already closed station. Note the variety of cars waiting at the level crossing, ranging from a posh Rover, whose driver seems to be a little impatient, a Ford Anglia in front of the lorry, a couple of Mark 1 Ford Cortinas, and a much older Morris at the head of the queue. Note the tail fins on the Vauxhall Cresta in the station drive to the left.

Just a hump in Derby Road is the only indication that a level crossing was once situated here. Note the white house on the right, whose roof line matches that in the same location in the earlier scene. On the far side of the road the distant chimney pots also have a familiar look to them. The front gardens of the new houses opposite are roughly where the Burton-bound platform ended, which is relevant to the next pair of photographs. *Phil Waterfield/GD*

BURTON-UPON-TRENT, HORNINGLOW (DERBY ROAD) LEVEL CROSSING: Stanier 'Black 5' 4-6-0 No 44813 storms across Horninglow level crossing in 1964 with, according to the headcode, an excursion to the Eastern Region, probably Skegness. Note the canopy of the station platform opposite, which had already been closed some 15 years earlier in 1949, and Holy Trinity Church in the background.

The new houses seen in the previous pair of photographs stand on the station site. It is likely that the original photograph was taken from the equivalent of the garden or front room of the property *(in the previous picture)* with the estate agent's board outside. The large silos at the Coors' Brewery can be seen in the distance. Holy Trinity Church was, perhaps surprisingly, demolished some time ago. *Phil Waterfield/GD*

**BURTON-UPON-TRENT, HORNINGLOW BRANCH:** This branch ran for less than a mile from a junction on the main line, close to Little Burton Bridge. Access to the branch, which was opened by the Midland Railway in 1873, was from the north and in its short length it had no fewer than four level crossings, at Derby Street, Victoria Street, Dallow Road and Victoria Crescent. It is at the latter crossing that we again see 'Jinty' No 47643 at the head of a rake of mineral wagons during 1963. It must be either lunch or 'knocking off' time judging by the impatient cyclists eager to be on their way. In the background is the former Cooper's Crescent Brewery. Another railway also existed here, a horse-drawn system that crossed Victoria Crescent at a point just beyond the existing lines, and was removed soon after the Midland branch opened.

There does seem to be some debate as to the course of the railway, judging by the attitude of the three gentlemen on the left. It actually ran behind them, and the new industrial unit stands roughly where the brewery was once located. Note the patch of cobblestones where the trio are standing, which corresponds with the cobbled entrance to the left of the level crossing in the earlier scene. The branch closed on 1 January 1970. *Phil Waterfield/ GD*

NEAR STRETTON AND CLAY MILLS: The North Staffordshire route from Burton-upon-Trent headed north for Dove Junction; there the tracks separated, with one line continuing to Stoke-on-Trent while the other curved around in a virtual semi-circle to rejoin the Midland main line at Willington Junction. 'Black 5' No 45335 is seen on the section south of Stretton & Clay Mills on the approach to Stretton Junction with a returning excursion, probably from Alton Towers, on 19 May 1964. Note the house next to the running lines on the left, which is believed to have been the crossing-keeper's residence.

The course of the railway is now occupied by Princess Way, and the overbridge carrying the busy A38 is just behind the photographer. The crossing-keeper's house remains, but now painted white. The avenue of trees on the right more accurately corresponds with the course of the railway, since in order to pinpoint the location of the crossing-keeper's house this viewpoint is slightly wider than the earlier scene. *Phil Waterfield/JW*

STRETTON & CLAY MILLS: The LCGB 'Midland Limited Rail Tour' passes through the station on 14 October 1962 with Class 'J11/3' 0-6-0 No 64354 at the head. The tour had originated at London Marylebone and had toured the East Midlands with a combination of Classes 'B16', 'J11', Johnson Class 3F, 'Black 5' and unrebuilt 'Patriot' power before returning to London St Pancras. The Class 'J11/3' had taken over the train at Nottingham Victoria from Class 'B16' No 61438, and hauled it via Eggington Junction to hand over to ex-Midland Railway Johnson Class 3F 0-6-0 No 43658 at Burton-upon-Trent. It had been a busy weekend for No 64354 as it had hauled a 'J11 Farewell Special' from Lincoln to Peterborough the previous day. Stretton & Clay Mills station had already been closed for 13 years by this date and the line's passenger service had also been discontinued some two years earlier. However the station remains in good condition, and even retains its name boards.

The line at this point ran through a shallow cutting, which has now been filled it. A linear walkway follows the course of the railway, with the position of the road (and the removed road bridge) being indicated by the barriers at the end of the pathway. *Phil Waterfield/JW*

ROLLESTON-ON-DOVE was the third station on the stretch of the North Staffordshire route between Burton and Dove Junction, and, like its two neighbours it closed in 1949. It was situated just to the south of Dove Junction, the latter forming a triangle with Eggington Junction. It was an interesting stretch of railway, as the western and northern chords were North Staffordshire metals, while the easterly chord belonged to the Great Northern and formed part of its route from Derby Friargate. On a grey day in 1963, Fowler Class 4F 0-6-0 No 44414 hammers through Rolleston-on-Dove station with a returning excursion, probably from Alton Towers. Note here too that the station buildings and name boards have survived long after closure.

The raised ground on each side of the picture indicates roughly where the platforms were positioned. The only tangible connection between the two scenes is the retaining wall on the right which has survived the passage of time, the wall was necessary, as the platforms were positioned on a slight embankment at this point. *Phil Waterfield/JW*

# INDEX OF LOCATIONS